BREAKTHROUGH
Series 1

For those committed to never going back...

GWEN SHAMBLIN

Copyright © 2008 by Gwen Shamblin
and The Weigh Down Workshop

The Weigh Down Workshop name and logo are registered trademarks. The *BREAKTHROUGH Series* name and logo are trademarks.

All rights reserved. No part of this publication may be stored in a retrieval system, transmitted, or reproduced in any way, including but not limited to photocopy, photograph, magnetic or other record, without the prior agreement and written permission of the publisher.

Art & cover design by Gwen Shamblin,
assisted by Ryan McCauley and Erin Shamblin

Printed in the United States of America
Remnant Publishing

Weigh Down Ministries
308 Seaboard Lane, Franklin, TN 37067
1-800-844-5208
www.weighdown.com
www.remnantfellowship.org

ISBN # 1-892729-04-0

BREAKTHROUGH™

A series that changes lives permanently!

This Book Belongs to: _____

Weigh Down Ministries ✝

A note from Weigh Down Ministries/Remnant Fellowship Churches around the world: the sale of this literature is not for a profit. This ministry is supported by Remnant Fellowship Churches around the world. The money is used for the print and duplication of materials, and any additional money is returned to God's ministry to reprint, reproduce, or produce other life-changing materials.

Every year, thousands of hurting people are given this material through seminars, books and other audio/video products absolutely free. In addition to this, all of the products are priced well under market value. With this in mind, all donations help get this message of hope and truth out to those without hope. Whether it is a few additional dollars on top of your purchase or a larger donation, all of the proceeds are used to teach people how to have a relationship with God and to love Him with all of their heart, soul, mind and strength.

These revelations and the Word of God are not for sale. They are freely given to those who cannot afford to pay for the reprinting of these words and videos and audios that are used solely for the furthering of the Kingdom of the One and Only God of the Universe. May they be used to make His True Nature known so that all will lovingly bow down to Him, and with great adoration, praise Him forever and ever. Amen.

He gives strength to the weary and increases the power of the weak. Even youths grow tired and weary, and young men stumble and fall; but those who hope in the LORD will renew their strength. They will soar on wings like eagles; they will run and not grow weary, they will walk and not be faint.

Isaiah 40:29-31

General Medical Information

You may have joined this program because the stronghold of food [or other addictions] is having a physical impact on your body. If this is the case, we recommend that you consult your physician for a medical examination before you begin. Also, if you have any preexisting health conditions, please continue to be under your physician's care and guidelines for food and medication. If you are enrolled in this seminar, it is assumed that you have been through Weigh Down Basics/Change classes and read the corresponding material regarding general medical guidelines and overdependence on medications. For more detailed information, please contact the Weigh Down office or see your original workbook materials.

Welcome!!!
To those committed to never going back!

TABLE OF CONTENTS

FOREWORD		...8
WEEK ONE	Committed to Never Going Back	...23
WEEK TWO	Let Go of Control	...55
WEEK THREE	A Relationship with God	...73
WEEK FOUR	Using Your Power vs. God's Power	...101
WEEK FIVE	For This Hour	...123
WEEK SIX	Don't Focus on the Body	...143
WEEK SEVEN	Purposeful Responsibility	...163
WEEK EIGHT	Breakthrough Moments	...183
APPENDIX	Weigh Down	...202
	Breakthrough Photos	...203
	Resources	...206

Foreword

Dear Seekers,

Welcome to a revolutionary weight loss program that has withstood the test of time and has yielded permanent results. Through the Weigh Down Workshop seminars and the best-selling original book, *The Weigh Down Diet*, this program has reached millions, and the statistics are unprecedented. These results are not to be found at any medical clinic or weight loss facility in the world. Any program can possibly produce a few testimonies of people who happened to lose weight, but no other program has produced hundreds of testimonies of those who have kept large amounts of weight off for over three, five, or even ten years! Yes, something is very different here, and it should give you much hope!

As you have learned in the basic teachings of the Weigh Down seminars, we are born with a void—a void that God placed inside of us so that we would search for Him and find Him. To satisfy these deep-down feelings, needs, or desires of the heart, we may often turn to food to fill this emptiness we all experience; however, trying to feed a hurting, needy heart with food or anything on this earth [alcohol, tobacco, antidepressants, sexual lusts, money, the praise of other people, etc.] is a common error. The person who attempts to feed a longing heart with food will stay on the path to overweight. Those who pursue an overindulgence of alcohol or tobacco or power will also reap the consequences of those pursuits. There is nothing inherently evil about food, alcohol, tobacco, money, credit cards, etc., however, it is wrong to become a slave to any of these things or to let them master you. Ultimately, it is the transfer of a relationship with the food over to a relationship with God that stops your greed, which results in weight loss.

Now it is time to take personal accountability and responsibility for your condition and go all the way–giving up any last bit of greed, control, or anti-authority that you have allowed to stay around. There is something inside the heart of men that loves control and wants to control both the things and the people around them. In this series, you will learn how to let go of that control and become completely committed to God ruling your life. You will learn to stop projecting or blaming others or blaming circumstances for your overeating, grazing, bingeing, late-night rendezvous with food, overspending, overdrinking, or other strongholds in your life. God gives this self-control as a part of the fruit of having access to His Spirit [Galatians 5]. You will learn to wait on God for everything and to wait on His Spirit to lead you every day. You will find your breakthrough moment when you know you are committed to never going back to your old ways of control, to dieting, to controlling your spouse, or to any type of greed for more than you have been given. You will learn how to stop going to food for sensual indulgence, escape, spacing out, a tranquilizing effect, comfort, and so on, and instead start swallowing regular foods only when your stomach growls [a cue for physical hunger]. And the result?...You will find yourself losing weight again!

All of the Weigh Down seminars, including this *BREAKTHROUGH Series*, are supported with personal counseling by those who have been successful, as well as with plentiful encouragement through books, internet radio, live webcasts, and other printed and audio materials. This seminar is also used for other addictions. Thousands have laid down cigarettes, overconsumption of alcohol, pornography, etc. with these principles. Each week in this class, you will watch a video with your fellow participants and then use this book and corresponding audios to stay focused throughout the week. [Before starting, please read the General Medical Information in the front of this book. If you have any questions about your materials, please call the Weigh Down office—the staff would love to help you!] Attending class each week will be essential for your journey. You will always want to watch out for satan's tricks to try and keep you from getting to these powerful, life-changing lessons [example: your computer breaks down, your kids get sick, etc.]. Remember that you have your class coordinator, your regional representative, the Weigh Down office staff, and the shepherds at Remnant Fellow-

BREAKTHROUGH

ship Churches as lifelines on this journey. We are here because God has worked mightily in our lives through God's ministry and we love to share and help others on this same path! Do not hesitate to email or call; we love to hear from you!

We are praying that each of you will find this breakthrough in your relationship with God and will experience the peace that is the result of surrendering all control to the Creator.

Committed to God

CONFESSION & COMMITMENT

Dear Seekers,

God has called us to penitence and repentance and confession and then to walk in newness of life. I am so grateful to have another day—I mean this more every day that I live.

Confession has two meanings. One is the confession that we make when we come to Christ and to God to worship Him alone. Most make this at their baptism. It should then be accompanied by obedience to what you vowed before the God of the Universe, and you should not let your words fall to the ground. First Timothy 6:12 says, "Fight the good fight of the faith. Take hold of the eternal life to which you were called when you made your good confession in the presence of many witnesses."

To me, it is a very serious matter not to keep your oath to God. But if you have failed unintentionally, then there must be repentance with a new confession.

So a second meaning is to admit [confess] that you have missed the path, and this is usually done before a godly spiritual leader and God. It is a formal admission of one's sins with repentance and the desire to never return to that behavior again. This type of religious obligation has been recorded from the earliest of days... "They stood where they were and read from the Book of the Law of the LORD their God for a quarter of the day, and spent another quarter in confession and in worshiping the LORD their God." Nehemiah 9:2-3

First, there must be repentance to a godly spiritual leader, and then if there is persistence of sin—the church. Matthew 18:15-18 says, "If your brother sins against you, go and show him his fault, just between the two of you. If he listens to you, you have won your brother over. But if he will not listen, take one or two others along, so that 'every matter may be established by the testimony of two or three witnesses.' If he refuses to listen to them, tell it to the church; and if he refuses to listen even to the church, treat him as you would a pagan or a tax collector. I tell you the truth, whatever you bind on earth will be bound in heaven, and whatever you loose on earth will be loosed in heaven."

Over the years, God's leaders have confronted and loved many a soul who has refused to listen. God's church, if it is to remain pure and if it is to follow the commands and wishes of the Most High God, must carry out

Committed to God

the will of God concerning pure greed and stubbornness.

If you know that you need to make a public confession or a confession or admittance of continual sin, do not delay. You must let God know as soon as possible that you intend to obey Him alone, while God is allowing ears to hear, eyes to see, and mouths to confess. It is time.

This must be done so that men will not be confused and know the good path and therefore be able to praise our God. Second Corinthians 9:13 is clear... "Because of the service by which you have proved yourselves, men will praise God for the obedience that accompanies your confession of the gospel of Christ, and for your generosity in sharing with them and with everyone else."

It is time to break through the old, crusty ground and rise to walk a new life!! Romans 6:4 says, "We were therefore buried with him through baptism into death in order that, just as Christ was raised from the dead through the glory of the Father, we too may live a new life."

Write out your confession and sign your commitment to God. You must put a bookmark here and come to this page first *every day* and pray and recommit to never going back to a controlling, greedy, miserable life. May God rule your whole day!

Confession:

Commitment: I am committed to putting God first and above all.

Signed:

"YOU WERE TAUGHT, WITH REGARD TO YOUR FORMER WAY OF LIFE, TO PUT OFF YOUR OLD SELF, WHICH IS BEING CORRUPTED BY ITS DECEITFUL DESIRES; TO BE MADE NEW IN THE ATTITUDE OF YOUR MINDS; AND TO PUT ON THE NEW SELF, CREATED TO BE LIKE GOD IN TRUE RIGHTEOUSNESS AND HOLINESS."
EPHESIANS 4:22-24

Committed to God
COMMITTED

A person committed to doing things God's way is a person who is done with dieting.

A person committed to doing things God's way is a person who will wait for the growl.

A person committed to doing things God's way is a person who will wake up to one alarm clock.

A person committed to doing things God's way is a person who gets right back up when they stumble.

A person committed to doing things God's way is a person who removes situations or foods from their life that have historically made them stumble.

A person committed to doing things God's way is a person who will not count calories.

A person committed to doing things God's way is a person who will not let the scale dictate their behavior.

A person committed to doing things God's way is a person who will not control their day.

A person committed to doing things God's way is a person who admits to greed and anti-authority.

Curses for Disobedience

Use this space for the unfortunate times that you take your eyes off of God. Make this a frequented page. It will turn you around before you binge.

BLESSINGS FOR OBEDIENCE

Start a list of the wonderful blessings you will reap by turning to God, as well as a list of the pain that you have felt as a result of the consequences of overeating or dieting. Read Deuteronomy 28.

BREAKTHROUGH

Breakthrough Convictions

What has been the biggest revelation that hit your heart this week from the video? This is called a **BREAKTHROUGH CONVICTION**. Write this out and collect them over the next eight weeks.

Breakthrough Lifestyle Changes

When you make a small or big change in your lifestyle from these convictions it is called a BREAKTHROUGH LIFESTYLE CHANGE.

BREAKTHROUGH Series

Seven Points That Stop the Binge:

- I AM IN A COMMITTED CLASS FOR GOD ALMIGHTY.
- I AM TO BE "BORN AGAIN" TO BE UNDER GOD'S CONTROL.
- I CANNOT GO TO HEAVEN AND BE A CONTROLLER.
- CONTROLLING IS THE SAME AS THE SINFUL NATURE.
- I'M NOT A GOOD BOSS. I'M NOT A GOOD EMPLOYER OF THIS BODY.
- MY OWN DESIRES HAVE ONLY LED TO LUST OF THE FLESH, LUST OF THE EYE, AND THE PRIDE OF LIFE.
- I AM READY TO MAKE A CHOICE TO GIVE UP MY CONTROL AND FOLLOW GOD'S LEAD.

    WRITE OUT THE NUMBER ON THE SCALES THAT YOU WILL WEIGH IF YOU BINGE: _____

    HOW LONG WILL IT TAKE FOR YOU TO GET THOSE EXTRA POUNDS OFF: _____

cutout

BREAKTHROUGH Series

Seven Points That Stop the Binge:

- I am in a committed class for God Almighty.
- I am to be "Born Again" to be under God's control.
- I cannot go to Heaven and be a controller.
- Controlling is the same as the sinful nature.
- I'm not a good boss. I'm not a good employer of this body.
- My own desires have only led to lust of the flesh, lust of the eye, and the pride of life.
- I am ready to make a choice to give up my control and follow God's lead.

  Write out the number on the scales that you will weigh if you binge: _____

  How long will it take for you to get those extra pounds off: _____

Cut these out and keep in your kitchen and wallet or purse.

BREAKTHROUGH Series

Seven Points That Stop the Binge:

- I am in a committed class for God Almighty.
- I am to be "Born Again" to be under God's control.
- I cannot go to Heaven and be a controller.
- Controlling is the same as the sinful nature.
- I'm not a good boss. I'm not a good employer of this body.
- My own desires have only led to lust of the flesh, lust of the eye, and the pride of life.
- I am ready to make a choice to give up my control and follow God's lead.

  Write out the number on the scales that you will weigh if you binge: _____

  How long will it take for you to get those extra pounds off: _____

Series™
changes lives permanently!
BreakthroughSeries.org
WeighDown.com
800-844-5208

Series™
changes lives permanently!
BreakthroughSeries.org
WeighDown.com
800-844-5208

Weight Record

The *BREAKTHROUGH* class is all about truth, and by getting on the scales and weighing each week, you will start telling yourself the truth. Stomach hunger is obeying God. Head hunger is obeying <u>self</u>, greed and your own desire to control or feed indulgence. Obey God and bow down to nothing else!

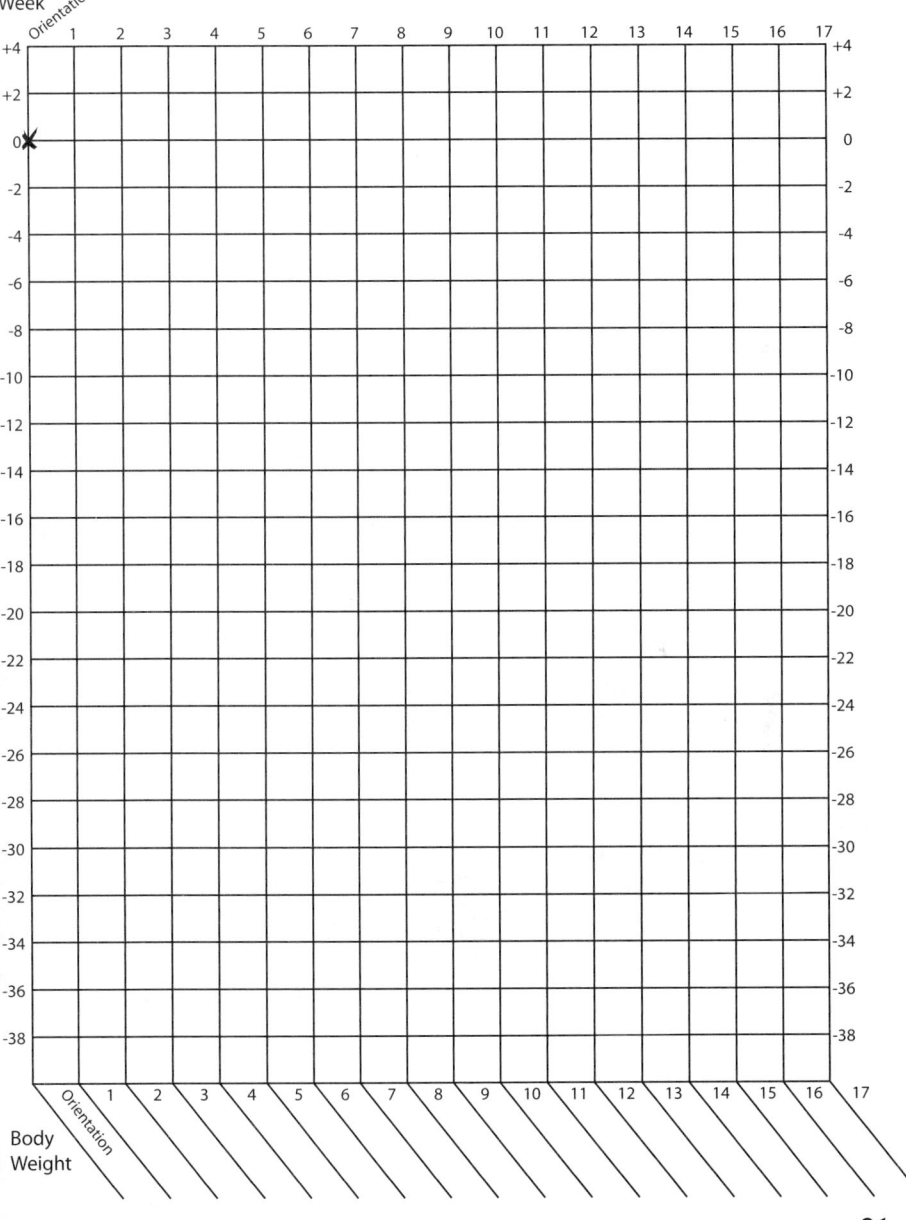

Weekly Checklist

- ☐ Read your "Confession & Commitment" page every day
- ☐ Watch Video One in class
- ☐ Listen to Audio One
- ☐ Add to your Breakthrough Convictions & Breakthrough Lifestyle Changes Charts
- ☐ Add to your Blessings for Obedience & Curses for Disobedience Charts
- ☐ Make notes in your *BREAKTHROUGH* Journal
- ☐ Answer Week One Daily Thought Questions
- ☐ Use your Reinforcement Resources & Truth Cards
- ☐ Fill in your Hour By Hour Chart
- ☐ Journal your Answered Prayers
- ☐ As you feel led, fill out the Weight Chart

Reinforcement Resources

- ☐ Get a new *BREAKTHROUGH Journal* to journal your answered prayers
- ☐ *The Tablet* — Read chapter 5 entitled "Why Is It Hard To Stop Eating"
- ☐ *Exodus Out of Egypt* — Listen to original Audio 12 entitled "Getting Back on Track"
- ☐ *Rise Above* — Read Chapter 1 entitled "A Passionate People"
- ☐ *Legend to The Treasure* Soundtrack — Listen to "Empty"
- ☐ *Laying Down Your Idols Devotional* — Read October 8th "A Treasured Passion"
- ☐ *Constant Encouragement* — Listen to "Getting Back up" Year 2, Volume 11

Scriptures

- ☐ Mark 12:28-29
- ☐ Ephesians 5:5
- ☐ Isaiah 66:2
- ☐ John 3:1-5
- ☐ I Peter 4:1-2
- ☐ Psalm 103:1-5
- ☐ Matthew 17:20

Lesson One
Committed to Never Going Back

This is a class that God has sent from the Heavens, and it will help you to finally break through the chains that have held you back. This class is for those ready to make the final choice to never going back. It is for those who hate the curses of overeating and any form of greed and want nothing but a peaceful, blessed life. You need to know that this class is not for beginners, but rather for people who have been through other Weigh Down classes and still need more. It is going to take your full or complete concentration. You will need to surrender your full heart and entire soul; it will take all of your entire mind and thought process and all of your energy and strength.

Any resistance to God should always get your total attention—FULL, COMPLETE ATTENTION. THIS MUST BE YOUR ONLY GOAL, YOUR NEW GOAL, YOUR NEW LEASE ON LIFE, HOW YOU ARE BORN AGAIN. This will be a full focus on obedience to God. Everyone left in this class believes that they can manage still flirting with the world and getting a relationship with God, and you are now miserable because you have neither. You feel guilty going to the world, but you still want it and God, too. *BREAKTHROUGH* is about making a choice and dropping one or the other. You need to make a choice and get off the fence.

You are going to return to the basics: eating when you are hungry and stopping when you are full. It is back to the first lessons of Weigh Down: hunger and fullness. There must be true hunger and the feeling of a growl. There must be polite satiation or fullness and no binge eating. We are going to deny head hunger, and we are going to replace that with stomach hunger. We must go from hunger to hunger. You will stop with a small amount when you feel satisfied. If you mess up and eat beyond full, you cannot eat again until you are hungry and you must stop upon the first bit of satisfaction.

This is all about something much more important than the food; it is about your whole life and direction. GREED is an ugly thing, and when there is greed, there is no faith in God; and therefore you do not rely on God during greedy binges. Hunger and fullness is just the right amount for you. It is totally the will of the Father, and there is nothing else for you to concentrate on. Ending greed will be the goal in the *BREAKTHROUGH Series*.

You must associate the growl with a relationship with God. You must associate stopping when you are full with a relationship with God in a "surrendered to authority" relationship. What you have not connected in the past and what has held you back from breaking free is that greed with food is idolatry. It is totally wrong—totally wrong. Keep this *BREAKTHROUGH Series* simple. It is time to start over—start over with a new way to eat and live. First of all, you've got to get down on your face and confess and cry out to God once more: "God, I want your Spirit over mine. God, I want your rule over mine."

I have noticed that there is a common thread among people who do not easily lose their weight. They put their hope in dieting. Don't be afraid to let go. Let go of control and have some faith. Why have faith in yourself? You are overweight still and you have more love for the food than ever as a result of controlling. You cannot control God, and He's not going to let you. The created cannot boss the Creator around. Stop talking back to God and stop making excuses.

LESSON 1

CRUCIAL FUNDAMENTALS

We will be returning to the crucial fundamentals each week. Does that seem insulting to you? Why? Think about it. Do not feel bad if you have to go back through each of the basic principles over and over. You are on the verge of the most critical, vital, pivotal and urgent thing in the world—not just the world, but for the eternal universe. Another fact: you are running out of time.

So, what is this essential fundamental? We must be born again. But to be born again is not a physical thing, but rather a spiritual thing. The concept is as follows: cease controlling your day with food or anything else and follow the lead of God.

Yes! But of course... Jesus said that we cannot enter the Kingdom of God unless we are born again. Why is this not talked about more? What does it mean? Why does something so simple seem impossible to get? It is because this pivotal truth is a fundamental concept that is blocked by a complicated and entangled set of attacks and blocks by the enemy. I have never in my life seen the like of distractions by satanic forces so that you miss this central message: we must walk daily with God by the leading of His Spirit. Satan's whole goal is to trip you up from obeying the Spirit of God. Satan does not want you to walk with God hour by hour; therefore, using the "Hour By Hour" chart or achieving a constant attention to the will of God each hour of the day, and especially at mealtime, will be highly attacked.

Open up your eyes to the fact that an entire evil kingdom is focused: they have one goal for the day, and that is to make sure that you do not hear, see, feel, or find God for the day. What is this lead of God? Week One of a basic Weigh Down class or Chapter One of *The Tablet* book is clear: eat only when you are physiologically hungry and deny all other urges to eat, deny all of your own desires to eat; deny head hunger. Keep it simple. You can only eat when your stomach is hungry, and you can only eat until you are politely satisfied. But notice that even if you do break through the distractions and sense the lead of God, these evil spirits will make sure that you get distracted so that you forget or miss the Spirit of God.

Something will divert you. You get to the scales and see that once again you must have missed the lead of God or otherwise you would have lost weight.

The purpose of this series is to help you to put an end to your life of dictating and controlling God, and instead, help you begin your life of following God all day long. You will be rethinking and analyzing every hour of your day. How could the most fundamental and essential or cardinal purpose of your life be lost by distractions? The war is powerful, and people do not even know what they are up against. There are so many spirits out there, and they talk through people or whisper in your ear. Truth is the weapon that breaks through the lies. How could truth not be used daily and several times per day along with constant pleading and prayer? These are not just simple truths—these are crucial fundamentals that you must be robbed of every day of your life or else you would not be overweight. It will require all of this to be able to take every thought captive and make it obedient to God. Please let these repetitive but paramount basics be reviewed each and every hour and each and every day until you are a new person—until you are entirely born again and walking hour by hour in God's Spirit—until you completely break away, break through, and rise to walk in a new life!

Again, God ruling your life in everything and especially in the food intake MUST BE YOUR ONLY GOAL. It is time to be BORN AGAIN. With a full heart and full focus, you can stop obeying yourself and obey God. This is God First AND God Alone! Slow down and turn your worries, interests, and desires toward God, His Kingdom, and His Will.

RETURN TO THE BASICS—THE WEIGH DOWN APPROACH

With God's help you can learn to stop in the middle of a meal and have no desire to eat the second half if your stomach is satisfied! God did not put chocolate or lasagna or real blue cheese dressing on earth to torture us, but rather for our enjoyment. However, He wants us to learn how to rise above the magnetic pull of the refrigerator so that food does not consume our lives!

Lesson 1

The problem and the solution

We have been created with two empty, needing-to-be-fed holes in our body. One is the stomach, and the other is the heart.

The *stomach* is a literal hole in our body which is to be fed with the proper amount of food. As for the *heart*, I am speaking figuratively of our deep-down feelings. To satisfy these deep-down feelings, needs, or desires of the heart, we may often turn to food and overload our stomach with more than it needs.

Figure 1-1: God created two empty places in each of us.

Trying to feed a hurting, needy heart with food or anything on this earth [alcohol, tobacco, antidepressants, sexual lusts, money, the praise of other people, etc.] is a common error. The person who attempts to feed a longing heart with food will stay on the path to overweight. Those who pursue an overindulgence of alcohol or tobacco or power will also reap the consequences of those pursuits. There is nothing inherently evil about food, alcohol, tobacco, money, credit cards, etc. However, it is wrong to become a slave to any of these things or to let them master you.

Figure 1-2: Feed the stomach only when it growls and stop feeding when it is satisfied (not stuffed). Using food to fill the heart leads to overweight.

The solution for overweight

As you can see from the diagram, we have been trying to feed our hurting, longing hearts with physical food. We have also learned

27

to love food. Therefore, the solution is as follows:

1. Relearn how to feed the stomach only when it is truly hungry.
2. Relearn how to feed or nourish the longing human soul with a relationship with God.
3. Relearn how to recognize the different "hunger" urges and not confuse them.

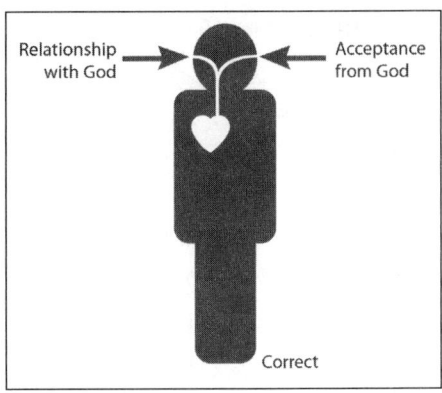

Figure 1-3: Our heart and needs are fed by looking for and finding that God is our Financier, Comforter, Mechanic, Lawyer, Physician, Counselor, Friend, Husband, Defender, Trusting Leader, and Father.

AM I A FAILURE?

Your major concerns will be: "How can this work for me? Because:
1. "I feel a distance between God and me because I thought He made me overweight and, for years, has not answered my prayers to take this weight off."
2. "I've tried every diet five times, every diet pill and exercise, and failed miserably—so how can this work?"

What we are really asking is... "Am I a failure, or is God angry at me and sabotaging me?"

Well, you are not a failure, it is not genetic, and God is not sabotaging you. He does hope that your slavery to diets and overweight will make you call out to Him. He is in love with you, and He wants you to depend on Him for deliverance so you can see how mighty He is and how important you are to Him.

Why have diets not worked so far? The reason is that you [like me and the rest of the world] have tried using man-made rules [diets] instead of God's rules. God has never asked anyone to eat food off of a list, to count fat exchanges, or to take an appetite suppressant. You have just been applying the wrong medicine to this condition. You were using your willpower and man's rules. God is too smart to let a local weight-loss group or fat gram counting be your ***Savior*** and thereby get all the credit. Man-made rules will not work.

Now, welcome to the Weigh Down Workshop, a place that teaches you God's rules for eating and shows you the futility of man-made rules. Welcome to the Weigh Down Workshop, a place that shows you how to use God's strength rather than your willpower! Welcome to the Weigh Down Workshop, a place where thousands of people are now thin after years of trying.

In summary: ***you are not a failure***. You have been using man's rules and your willpower, and now you are going to use God's plan for eating and His strength. There is hope, and God will get the credit!

Diets will never work

Diets do not get to the root of the problem. In fact, diets aggravate the problem rather than alleviate it. Diets just boil down to making the food behave. Food companies have spent several decades and millions of dollars to pull out the fat and calories so that the food is righteous! Actually, billions of dollars are spent by the food industry to make us feel needy. Many food companies may not want us to succeed in losing weight, but, rather, would prefer to make us feel dependent on them so we will consume whatever is sold. In fact, the more diets fail, the better off the industry is.

The root of the problem is not the food ingredients, but how much volume is going down the old hatch [our esophagus]! And, indeed, we consumers have wanted the food industry to take the fat out of the Twinkie so that we can simply eat more Twinkies. Changing the food but not changing the volume of what is swallowed will leave us on a roller coaster of weight loss and weight gain. Changing our metabolism or our nervous system by taking pills and hormones is not permanent, because we cannot stay on them because of the side effects. The motivation to be thin is not vanity—it is natural. God has programmed us to want the best for our bodies.

We cannot continue to have the doctor suck out the fat from one part of the body [suction-assisted lipectomies] while we continue to stuff our mouths. We must surrender the root of the problem; that is so much easier to do than diets or surgery. Weigh Down is different from all other diet systems because it is not selling a diet plan, a food, or whatever. It is selling a future, a future to be filled and fulfilled. Hunger is filled, God's love is embraced and enjoyed, and appetites are under control and given to God.

Do you have to be religious to do the program?

For those of you who do not feel particularly religious—do not worry. You have exactly what you need to be able to do this program. You see, each of us has a heart to worship, and we all adore something. That tells us we have the capacity to give our heart to something. The question is: can you transfer your devotion from one thing to another? The answer is: *yes!*

Giving our hearts over to something is a learned process and can be relearned. For example, some people *enjoy* sports, but other people seem to *worship* sports. Some people enjoy material things, but other people seem to worship things. Some people use money, but other people will do anything to get it.

Some people use food for fuel to run the body, and some people dream about food. Some of these dreamers have been known to get up in the morning and find the bony remains of fried chicken on their chest! This old relationship with food can be transferred to a relationship with God or to a heart for God.

In the past you may have loved the feeling of planning a binge and dreaming over recipes, cookbooks, and magazines that have food plans and pictures of food. You may have looked forward to the feeling of waiting for everyone to go to bed [and they had better not get back up out of bed] so you could prepare, cook, and consume the food without the judgment of anybody.

The good news is that you can relearn how to get that feeling from the Lord. When you learn to get this happy feeling from finding God, you will experience much more fulfillment. Bingeing out on seeking God has no yucky, guilty, depressing side effects. In other words, it is possible to let go of that old way of having fun and replace it with something so much more filling [yet with no calories!]. By choosing this new path you will lose weight and never regain the weight.

I know some of you are reading in disbelief. I can hear you thinking, "You're telling me that if I am not hungry and want to eat a pan of brownies, that I should go to the Bible and read it instead!?" This concept is not "pie in the sky." Keep reading. I dare you to let me prove this to you.

Thousands of people have taken the Weigh Down Workshop seminar or have read this book. They no longer get this "binge high" from food, but from focusing completely on our true Heavenly Father and trying to please Him. Jesus said, "My food is to do the will of Him who sent me and to finish His work" [John 4:34].

Some people have experienced a "high" when they became involved in exercise. While the "high" is not wrong, it is not complete. And usually, obsessive, tedious exercise to become thin eventually wears thin if the exercise is self-focused rather than God-focused. Exercise, like food, must also be put in its place and not worshiped, but enjoyed.

The transfer to a heavenly focus from a focus on food, exercise, or anything else is much more delightful and fulfilling. It has so many rewards that you will never want to return to giving your heart to anything else!

How do you lose weight?

Once you stop going to food for sensual indulgence, escape, spacing out, a tranquilizing effect, comfort, and so on, and start swallowing regular foods only when your stomach growls, you will swallow or eat just one-half to one-third of what you used to swallow. The *desire* eating goes away. That means you will lose weight! You will be able to do this; it happens naturally. You will not have to measure the food or count the grams—your stomach will guide you. The volume of food decreases as you focus on hunger and fullness. Thousands of ex-dieters are doing this within twenty-four hours of starting Weigh Down.

Amount of Food in 24 Hours

Before Weigh Down Workshop

Diets let you chew this much; therefore, the food content has to change to hay-like foods, optional calories, Styrofoam-like material, and fat-free, tasteless concoctions. **Volume** has not changed.

After Weigh Down Workshop

You will be eating 2/3 less fat, 2/3 less carbohydrates, 2/3 less protein, 2/3 less salt, etc., but every bite will be foods that you love!

Figure 1-4: Expect your food consumption to go down in this program—anywhere from one-half to two-thirds.

The typical weight-loss program suggests losing weight through diet and exercise. We suggest that if you lose the passion for food, the result will be that you eat less food and therefore lose weight permanently. The typical 1950s–1990s approach tried to fix the body or the food but did not address the passion. The Weigh Down Workshop approach fixes the heart first, and the body follows.

There is no other method except obedience to hunger and fullness that will set you free from the LOVE of food.

The Weigh Down Workshop will show you how God can bring us to peace with food—never to return to the nightmare of endless overweight, yo-yo dieting and "have-to" exercise regimens, but rather to a calm, nonmagnetized approach to regular foods with the ability to approach foods such as rich entrees and desserts without losing control. Exercise need no longer be connected to burning calories; instead it can be an enjoyable activity. You will be free!

LESSON 1

DAILY THOUGHT QUESTIONS

❏ What has been the biggest revelation that hit your heart this week from the video? This is called a...
        BREAKTHROUGH CONVICTION.
Write these out and collect them over the next eight weeks. Record them each week and rewrite them on the permanent Breakthrough Conviction Chart in the front of the book. You can have several of these convictions per week. Make sure to go over these every week. Even if it seems stupid [that is satan's whisper], write them down. *Example: I am finally realizing that the only way to lose weight is to wait for true hunger each time.*

❏ Now take this *Breakthrough Conviction* and make a change in your life. When you make a small or big change in your lifestyle from these convictions it is called a...
        BREAKTHROUGH LIFESTYLE CHANGE.
Record them each week and rewrite them on the permanent Breakthrough Lifestyle Change Chart in the front of the book. Praise God for them and make sure you note the weight lifted off of you because you are changing to obey God rather than Self.

❏ REPETITION OF SINS MUST STOP. You may not get another chance to get it right. What sin are you repeating, and what have you done today to stop that?

33

BLESSINGS FOR OBEDIENCE
- Praise God for the Breakthrough!!! Use this space to praise God for what He has done so far. Record these each week and rewrite them on the Blessings for Obedience Chart in the front of the book. How neat that the whole world is wonderful and life is worth living if we just focus on God for the day! *Example: I feel a heavy burden being lifted off my mind and body when I obey God.*

CURSES FOR DISOBEDIENCE
- Use this space for the unfortunate times that you take your eyes off of God. [Also rewrite them on the Curses for Disobedience Chart in the front of the book.] I have been at this for years, and I have seen that people are quick to forget the problems and curses that are caused by taking their eyes off of God. Make this a frequented page. It will turn you around before you binge.

- Did you deny head hunger this week? Did you eat with mouth hunger? Totally analyze your head hunger—with who, what, when, where, how, and why did it happen, and write this down.

Lesson 1

❏ Hour by hour is key to this class's goal: a relationship with God. Waiting for the growl is not about weight loss—it is about surrendering control so that you can have a relationship with God. Slow down. You need to take one hour at a time, one week at a time, one month at a time. If you think about it, you have 8 hours of sleep and 8 hours of working for someone else—where you should be—because you are paid to be focusing on someone else. If you are a stay-at-home mom, it is no different. You are working for your husband, and he wants you to cook, clean, do laundry and homeschool—and that is an 8-hour job at least! That adds up to 16 hours out of the 24 hours.

Now...concentrate on those last 8 hours. What are you doing with those last 8 hours? Fill in the following blanks with what you have been doing.

4:00 pm _____
5:00 pm _____
6:00 pm _____
7:00 pm _____
8:00 pm _____
9:00 pm _____
10:00 pm _____
11:00 pm _____

We have got to surrender the night hours. Now turn to the "Hour by Hour" Activity on page 46 to begin this process of keeping a NEW Spirit-led evening. Record what you do in your journal and rate it. Is it God-focused/Christ-focused? Or is it greedy/self-focused? Your goal is to surrender the last 8 hours of your day to your King.

BREAKTHROUGH Series

❏ Take the following space to fill out at least a 2-3 day food recall. It is very hard to remember what you put into your mouth, and it takes a lot of attention, so please be very focused and detailed.

❏ Extra time must be spent wisely. You must listen to and/or read this truth every single day. You have audios so that you can hear this over and over, because it is the lies that we must overcome. Lies are broken only with Truth. You cannot count on yourself right now. Your past thought process has caused overeating. You have bought into lies, or otherwise you would have lost the weight by now. You must LISTEN to the audios, READ the workbook, and READ the Word of God. Keep the truth nearby at all times and read/listen to it at every opportunity that you get—ESPECIALLY AT YOUR STRUGGLING HOURS.

❏ Write out WHICH HOURS you think you need to be re-focusing the most, and have a PLAN to use these Truth Resources at those hours.

❏ Did you get re-focused today by listening to an audio or by reading your workbook? What did you do? Which resource did you use? When did you do it?

❏ Learn to send yourself reminders/alerts on your phone [especially during those difficult hours]. It wouldn't hurt to get someone in the class to be your Accountability Partner, and you two could pray together each night. Your phone reminders could be as follows:
- "Growl to growl…give up control!"
- "Pray more!"
- "Remember the pain of greed."
- "If you end the greed, you will stop the overeating."

❏ DIETING has gotten you into a complicated mess, and it is NOT God's plan for your body. Write out how your past dieting has caused pain and problems in your life.

❏ People lie to themselves so that they can get away with extra eating. If you are telling yourself, "It's okay to go on and eat this once even though I'm not quite hungry or growling yet" or… "It's okay to go past full just this once. I'll get back on track tomorrow…"—then you are lying to yourself. Some other examples of lies you could be falling for are:
- "I will be empty/bored for the rest of the night if I don't get to spend the time eating food…"
- "This one time of overeating will not matter…"

- "I can go beyond full and just wait longer tomorrow to eat…"
- "I can overeat tonight and just fast tomorrow…"
- "Even if I gain a little bit of weight, I can get that back off…"
- "I'm tired. I'm hurting. I'm depressed. Food can comfort me."

Now write down the lies you fall for—the ones that you have listened to for years—and be familiar with them so that you can turn them OFF [refuse to believe them] when the situation comes back around!

LIE #1 _____

LIE #2 _____

LIE #3 _____

LIE #4 _____

LIE #5 _____

❏ What do you focus on when you come to class? Do not focus on the people who have not lost their weight, but rather focus on those who have. If need be, watch the "20,000 Pound Lineup" YouTube video [**www.youtube.com/watch?v=lwvaj1Dy_5A**] every day so that you can end the lies that say, "People cannot lay down the love of food… People cannot really permanently lose their weight… People cannot stop sinning." Stop and refocus. Look at all the people who were obese and now have been thin for two, five, and ten years! It CAN be done! People CAN wait for the stomach to growl. People CAN stop eating beyond full. Even little children stop when they are satisfied. Remember back…you used to do that when you were young. Go back and remember when you used to eat like a thin eater [or if you never did, then watch a child eat for a day…] and write out some examples here of HOW they wait for hunger, HOW they stop when they are satisfied or full, HOW they quickly go to the next event the moment they feel satisfied, and HOW they are simply NOT focused on the food at all—all day:

❑ You must show restraint, moderation, and temperance in your eating. If you've got weight to lose, it will probably be only 1-3 times per day in small amounts [with the exception of children and pregnant women]. You should eat slowly but without drawing the experience out longer than it should. What are some practical ways that you can show restraint at the table? List them all and put a check mark by ones you use. For example:

   ❑ Pray before the meal
   ❑ Slow down
   ❑ Interpose a delay in the middle of the meal
   ❑ Look up and visit with those around you
   ❑ Sip between bites
   ❑ Read a Truth Card in the middle of a meal
   ❑ Ask for a to-go box at the beginning of the meal so that you can get your food "out of sight, out of mind" as soon as you feel satisfied
   ❑ Instead of being the last person to finish, try being the first person to stop eating

BREAKTHROUGH

- ❏ According to the video, just as someone lets go of the steering wheel and says, "I'm not going to drive anymore"—you get up out of the car, walk around, and get in the passenger's seat. Let go of the steering wheel. If you can let go of driving the car and let someone else drive [with no "backseat commands"], then you can do the same with eating. God can drive your stomach. The only thing you need in the universe is God's Spirit. We are LUCKY and BLESSED to have Someone to tell us what to do!

- ❏ Do you feel like you are a controlling person? Use this space provided to confess to God how you have controlled Him and others. Use this space to repent and start over.

- ❏ The average person expects their child to obey. The average teacher expects the students to obey. The police expect compliance in full to the laws on the roads. Why is it so hard to obey God? According to the video, it is possible that you have been spoiled in life. It is also possible that you have completely missed the corrections and curses from disobedience. Think of situations where you have expected someone else to obey but have not expected that of yourself. Keep this list near and expect this from yourself this week. Now it is time to expect more of yourself. If others can obey you, then YOU can obey God! Every year we should be able to expect more out of our children

LESSON 1

and more out of ourselves. How have you spoiled yourself? List expectations that you should have of yourself at your age.
Example:
I am ___ years old. I should be able to wait for stomach hunger.
I am ___ years old. I should be able to stop at one glass of wine.

❏ These next two questions are on the BLESSINGS OF HEALTH that you receive when you eat less food.

How does it feel when you deny yourself extra food and mobilize the stored energy all over your body? Describe in detail how much energy you have when you wait on God and obey His amounts.

How does it feel when you keep eating, past full, as if for an overweight body instead of a thin body? Describe in detail how tired you are when you overeat. Please share these with your classmates online.

41

❑ Complications of Obesity/Related Diseases

Overweight and obese people are at an increased risk for developing the following conditions [in no particular order]:

- Type 2 [non-insulin dependent] diabetes
- Cardiovascular disease
- Stroke
- Hypertension
- Hypothyroidism
- Dyslipidemia
- Hyperinsulinemia, insulin resistance, glucose intolerance
- Congestive heart failure
- Angina pectoris
- Cholecystitis
- Cholelithiasis
- Osteoarthritis
- Gout
- Fatty liver disease
- Sleep apnea and other respiratory problems
- Polycystic ovary syndrome [PCOS]
- Fertility complications
- Pregnancy complications
- Psychological disorders
- Uric acid nephrolithiasis [kidney stones]
- Stress urinary incontinence
- Cancer of the kidney, endometrium, breast, colon and rectum, esophagus, prostate and gallbladder
- Death

❑ Here are 20 diseases or conditions related to Obesity:

1. Diabetes, a disorder where the pancreas is not producing enough, or sometimes not any, insulin. Diabetes can lead to a whole host of other medical issues, and obesity is one of the main causes.
2. Cancer has many different forms and types; many of them could be prevented with more attention to eating healthily and avoiding obesity.
3. Congestive heart failure is a condition in which your heart can't pump enough blood to your body's other organs.
4. Enlarged heart is another heart condition where the muscle of your heart becomes larger due to being overworked, which naturally happens if you are overweight.

5. Pulmonary embolism is a sometimes fatal blockage of an artery. Being overweight causes most people to reduce activity, and after time, lack of activity can result in an embolism.
6. Polycystic ovarian syndrome is a condition in which cysts develop in your ovaries. These can burst, causing even further problems.
7. Gastro-esophageal reflux disease happens when stomach acid and juices flow from your stomach back up into your esophagus. It is common in overweight people.
8. Fatty liver disease is a reversible condition in which large pockets of fat accumulate in liver cells.
9. A hernia is caused when the hole in the diaphragm weakens and enlarges.
10. Erectile dysfunction is the inability to develop or maintain an erection, which can be caused by a medical problem due to obesity.
11. Urinary incontinence is the inability to control urination. It is frequently associated with obesity, weak bladder and pelvic floor muscles.
12. Chronic renal failure, meaning your kidneys fail to work, is a much greater risk to those who are overweight or obese.
13. Lymph edema is a condition that occurs from a damaged or dysfunctional lymphatic system, sometimes caused by people suffering from obesity actually crushing their own lymphatics.
14. Cellulitis is a spreading infection, involving both the dermis and subcutaneous skin tissues, resulting from poor lymph flow caused by obesity.
15. Stroke is caused by a lack of blood supply to your brain.
16. Pickwickian syndrome is characterized by sleep apnea resulting from obesity placing an excessive load on your pulmonary system.
17. Depression is a condition where a person feels miserable constantly, even to the point of being suicidal. It can be worse for someone who also has a weight problem.
18. Osteoarthritis is a clinical syndrome in which low-grade inflammation results in pain in your joints. It is caused by abnormal wearing of the cartilage, oftentimes due to obesity.
19. Gout occurs when uric acid accumulates in your blood. Nerve endings then become irritated, causing extreme pain, which is made worse by carrying extra weight.
20. Gallbladder disease commonly affects overweight people as a result of high blood cholesterol levels, which cause gall stones.

BREAKTHROUGH

❏ According to a Surgeon General report, obesity is responsible for 300,000 deaths every year in the United States. Your homework this week is to watch the YouTube videos, "The World's Fattest Child" or "700 Pound Man." As America is getting larger and larger and more and more insensitive to hunger and fullness, they are getting more and more unhealthy. We are witnessing the first generation in over two centuries that has a shorter life expectancy than their parents.

❏ It would be unfortunate if God saw any sadness in you while you were denying yourself and obeying His will. No looking back like Lot's wife! Write down the consequences of sin or backsliding, and write down the rewards for moving forward! Look at the contrast! This is the Committed Class—let's break through!!

Consequences/Curses: *Rewards:*

❏ Do not be discouraged by anything in the past, but rather be happy and joyful that you have this chance! This is huge!! Read Psalms 103 and write out verses 1–5.

Prayer

To get started, you will need to humble yourself every day—every day—getting down and praying, "O God, I'm so sorry. Thank You for an opportunity to pray to You more, but God, I'm just praying that You forgive me, and thank You for this chance. O God, I don't want to do anything to hurt a relationship with You. Open my eyes to this incredible chance. Help me, God, to give up control."

So start with a prayer, and then get down an hour later and pray again, because satan will try to inject you with pride and fear to get you to return to taking over control with dieting. Yet you need to replace control with contriteness and dependence on the great decisions of God. It becomes a way of life.

Answered Prayers

You can break through into this freedom of being connected to God's Spirit hour by hour, by constant input, then constant praying, and then looking for the answered prayers. Through this obedience and these amazing answered prayers, the power is incredible; it is showing the world that we can move the mountains that Jesus was talking about [Matthew 17:20]. This will get you more and more excited about this relationship with God; and please, do not give up, because this is the coolest thing in the world when you finally connect. Write in your journal your answered prayers from this week.

Hour by Hour
Finding the Spirit of God

Waiting for God's lead every hour is so fun and rewarding. This can be through true hunger, or your husband or boss, or prayer for what to do to help someone else, etc. Use this chart, as you feel led, as a tool to help you get into this lifestyle of depending on God hour by hour, day by day, and week by week.

Day: Monday, January 23rd

Hour	Wait for God's lead?	Comments
6:00 AM	☑ Yes ☐ No	Woke up and prayed for God's lead.
7:00 AM	☑ Yes ☐ No	No hunger so got ready for the day.
8:00 AM	☑ Yes ☐ No	Prayed for focus as I drove to work, listened to class audio.
9:00 AM	☐ Yes ☐ No	
10:00 AM	☐ Yes ☐ No	
11:00 AM	☐ Yes ☐ No	
12:00 PM	☑ Yes ☐ No	Felt hunger, ate half of sandwich & a diet coke
1:00 PM	☐ Yes ☐ No	
2:00 PM	☐ Yes ☐ No	
3:00 PM	☐ Yes ☐ No	
4:00 PM	☑ Yes ☐ No	Got home, spent time with kids
5:00 PM	☐ Yes ☐ No	
6:00 PM	☑ Yes ☐ No	Prayed before dinner, did great!
7:00 PM	☐ Yes ☐ No	
8:00 PM	☑ Yes ☐ No	God led me to reach out to a hurting person, lifted my spirit!

BREAKTHROUGH *Series*

Day: _____

HOUR BY HOUR

Finding the Spirit of God

Hour	Wait for God's lead?	Comments
6:00 AM	☐ Yes ☐ No	
7:00 AM	☐ Yes ☐ No	
8:00 AM	☐ Yes ☐ No	
9:00 AM	☐ Yes ☐ No	
10:00 AM	☐ Yes ☐ No	
11:00 AM	☐ Yes ☐ No	
12:00 PM	☐ Yes ☐ No	
1:00 PM	☐ Yes ☐ No	
2:00 PM	☐ Yes ☐ No	
3:00 PM	☐ Yes ☐ No	
4:00 PM	☐ Yes ☐ No	
5:00 PM	☐ Yes ☐ No	
6:00 PM	☐ Yes ☐ No	
7:00 PM	☐ Yes ☐ No	
8:00 PM	☐ Yes ☐ No	
9:00 PM	☐ Yes ☐ No	
10:00 PM	☐ Yes ☐ No	
11:00 PM	☐ Yes ☐ No	
Middle of the night	☐ Yes ☐ No	

Could you have done a better job today? Explain.

BREAKTHROUGHSERIES.ORG   WEIGHDOWN.COM

BREAKTHROUGH Series

Day: _____

Hour by Hour

Finding the Spirit of God

Hour	Wait for God's lead?	Comments
6:00 AM	☐ Yes ☐ No	
7:00 AM	☐ Yes ☐ No	
8:00 AM	☐ Yes ☐ No	
9:00 AM	☐ Yes ☐ No	
10:00 AM	☐ Yes ☐ No	
11:00 AM	☐ Yes ☐ No	
12:00 PM	☐ Yes ☐ No	
1:00 PM	☐ Yes ☐ No	
2:00 PM	☐ Yes ☐ No	
3:00 PM	☐ Yes ☐ No	
4:00 PM	☐ Yes ☐ No	
5:00 PM	☐ Yes ☐ No	
6:00 PM	☐ Yes ☐ No	
7:00 PM	☐ Yes ☐ No	
8:00 PM	☐ Yes ☐ No	
9:00 PM	☐ Yes ☐ No	
10:00 PM	☐ Yes ☐ No	
11:00 PM	☐ Yes ☐ No	
Middle of the night	☐ Yes ☐ No	

Could you have done a better job today? Explain.

BreakthroughSeries.org   WeighDown.com

BREAKTHROUGH Series

Day: _____

HOUR BY HOUR

Finding the Spirit of God

Hour	Wait for God's lead?	Comments
6:00 AM	☐ Yes ☐ No	
7:00 AM	☐ Yes ☐ No	
8:00 AM	☐ Yes ☐ No	
9:00 AM	☐ Yes ☐ No	
10:00 AM	☐ Yes ☐ No	
11:00 AM	☐ Yes ☐ No	
12:00 PM	☐ Yes ☐ No	
1:00 PM	☐ Yes ☐ No	
2:00 PM	☐ Yes ☐ No	
3:00 PM	☐ Yes ☐ No	
4:00 PM	☐ Yes ☐ No	
5:00 PM	☐ Yes ☐ No	
6:00 PM	☐ Yes ☐ No	
7:00 PM	☐ Yes ☐ No	
8:00 PM	☐ Yes ☐ No	
9:00 PM	☐ Yes ☐ No	
10:00 PM	☐ Yes ☐ No	
11:00 PM	☐ Yes ☐ No	
Middle of the night	☐ Yes ☐ No	

Could you have done a better job today? Explain.

BREAKTHROUGHSERIES.ORG   WEIGHDOWN.COM

BREAKTHROUGH Series

Day: _____

HOUR BY HOUR

Finding the Spirit of God

Hour	Wait for God's lead?	Comments
6:00 AM	☐ Yes ☐ No	
7:00 AM	☐ Yes ☐ No	
8:00 AM	☐ Yes ☐ No	
9:00 AM	☐ Yes ☐ No	
10:00 AM	☐ Yes ☐ No	
11:00 AM	☐ Yes ☐ No	
12:00 PM	☐ Yes ☐ No	
1:00 PM	☐ Yes ☐ No	
2:00 PM	☐ Yes ☐ No	
3:00 PM	☐ Yes ☐ No	
4:00 PM	☐ Yes ☐ No	
5:00 PM	☐ Yes ☐ No	
6:00 PM	☐ Yes ☐ No	
7:00 PM	☐ Yes ☐ No	
8:00 PM	☐ Yes ☐ No	
9:00 PM	☐ Yes ☐ No	
10:00 PM	☐ Yes ☐ No	
11:00 PM	☐ Yes ☐ No	
Middle of the night	☐ Yes ☐ No	

Could you have done a better job today? Explain.

BREAKTHROUGHSERIES.ORG

WEIGHDOWN.COM

BREAKTHROUGH Series

Day: _____

HOUR BY HOUR

Finding the Spirit of God

Hour	Wait for God's lead?	Comments
6:00 AM	☐ Yes ☐ No	
7:00 AM	☐ Yes ☐ No	
8:00 AM	☐ Yes ☐ No	
9:00 AM	☐ Yes ☐ No	
10:00 AM	☐ Yes ☐ No	
11:00 AM	☐ Yes ☐ No	
12:00 PM	☐ Yes ☐ No	
1:00 PM	☐ Yes ☐ No	
2:00 PM	☐ Yes ☐ No	
3:00 PM	☐ Yes ☐ No	
4:00 PM	☐ Yes ☐ No	
5:00 PM	☐ Yes ☐ No	
6:00 PM	☐ Yes ☐ No	
7:00 PM	☐ Yes ☐ No	
8:00 PM	☐ Yes ☐ No	
9:00 PM	☐ Yes ☐ No	
10:00 PM	☐ Yes ☐ No	
11:00 PM	☐ Yes ☐ No	
Middle of the night	☐ Yes ☐ No	

Could you have done a better job today? Explain.

BREAKTHROUGHSERIES.ORG   WEIGHDOWN.COM

A Breakthrough Moment
The Night Lie

Satan has most people just where he wants them: deceived, year after year after year. You go to bed every night determined to be different. You get up every morning with the same resolve. You pray, and yet, at the end of the day and at the last minute you are presented by satan an opportunity to eat, and you make a rash decision. You have some thought that eating will be comforting and rest your body. You have some personal lie that grants you permission to either eat when you are not hungry or to eat beyond full. It allows you lust at night—just this one last time. This deceitful lie tells you to go ahead this time; it tells you that you can just eat a little and stop there. There will be no damage done. You go to bed disgusted and wake up to be different and believe that you will—so you don't feel too bad. Then you look up and you have listened to a circle of lies for 10, 20, 30 years or more. You are not changing. Your faith is not stronger.

But the truth is that you are not good at stopping when you are eating, because you were not hungry to start with; and if you are not hungry, then you are full. Where is full? You cannot find it when you are not hungry. You are feeding head hunger and greed, and greed has no satiation. You have to use your own willpower to stop, and for most, willpower is slowly disappearing, because you can't seem to stop anyway. You do not ask God in on a late-night binge—you try not to know that you are doing it yourself. You are trying to deceive even yourself—so you eat quickly. You feel you must take care of yourself, that the food might not be there for you. This day you are going to eat because tomorrow you are going to eat a lot less. But then you don't. After years of this, don't you see that you are deceived by a set of lies that work on you?

How could the same lies work on someone every day? How have you managed to binge every night and wake up every day resolved to be different yet are no different and if anything, greedier? How does someone fall for the lie at night? How could someone be

LESSON 1

so afraid to have a day that has less greed, less food, less lust, less shopping? What is this fear?

You need faith. You need some faith that God will take care of you in a different way. Pray for faith. End your fears and stop listening to the lies. You need to know that night lies come on fast and that they put pressure on you to move quickly so that you cannot think. The pressure is enormous in your mind to make a rash decision. You must fight this false rash pressure. It is not real—it is a test. Don't fall for this pressure lie, whatever it is: you will not see the food again, you must eat before anyone sees you, you might not get this chance again, etc. You must say "no" and see that you have plenty of food right there on your body. You have already packed on extra meals. Tell yourself the truth. Look into the mirror before you eat—not afterwards. LOOK INTO THE MIRROR BEFORE YOU EAT— NOT AFTERWARDS. This applies to overdrinking. You need to remember your night before and your embarrassing behavior before you drink, and don't count on this night being different. You need to look into your closet before you go shopping—not after. You say you're going to return it—but do you? You are afraid that you will need that article of clothing.

If you stop and see the truth about your bad track record and say no, you will be so blessed. Breakthrough! In just a few minutes you will find that God has given you a way of escape and a blessing. The Truth will set you free. Get your Truth Cards and Scripture ready. Why lie to yourself for another 10 to 20 years? Is that what you want? No! So stop lying, tell the truth to yourself when you hear the lie, and get skinny. The night lie is met with the night truth, and you will lose all your weight. Yeah! Notice that you typically weigh yourself in the mornings. Start weighing in at 5:00pm. Night truth— a new concept! We are going to break through the darkness!

A Servant of God,

53

Weekly Checklist

- ☐ Read your "Confession & Commitment" page every day
- ☐ Watch Video Two in class
- ☐ Listen to Audio Two
- ☐ Add to your Breakthrough Convictions & Breakthrough Lifestyle Changes Charts
- ☐ Add to your Blessings for Obedience & Curses for Disobedience Charts
- ☐ Make notes in your *BREAKTHROUGH* Journal
- ☐ Answer Week Two Daily Thought Questions
- ☐ Use your Reinforcement Resources & Truth Cards
- ☐ Fill in your Hour By Hour Chart
- ☐ Journal your Answered Prayers
- ☐ As you feel led, fill out the Weight Chart

Reinforcement Resources

- ☐ *BREAKTHROUGH* Truth Cards—Get a set for home and the car!
- ☐ *The Tablet*—Read chapter 11 entitled "Learning To Sense Internal Controls"
- ☐ *Laying Down Your Idols Devotional*—Read November 5th "Only a Day?"
- ☐ *The Tablet*—Read chapter 12 entitled "How To Have A Balanced Meal"
- ☐ *Constant Encouragement*—Listen to "Don't Mix the Message" Year 1, Volume 42"
- ☐ *Constant Encouragement*—Listen to "You were Never Called to Rule" Year 2, Volume 35

Scriptures

- ☐ Exodus 20:1-4
- ☐ I Corinthians 3:16-23
- ☐ Jeremiah 17:4-10
- ☐ Romans 8:1-26
- ☐ Psalms 38:15
- ☐ Isaiah 30:12-22
- ☐ John 14:1-3
- ☐ Galatians 5:22-25

Lesson Two
Let Go of Control

*T*he fruit of the Spirit is love, joy, peace, patience, kindness, goodness, faithfulness, gentleness, and self-control. I want to change the word "self-control" to "God-control."

Dieting and saying "yes" to dieting is wrong because it is person control vs. God control. The reason is because what you are REALLY saying is, "I am not going to let go of the food, and I am not committed to God ruling. I am going to maneuver around idolatry and stay with the food and the chewing and the amount of chewing. I am going to do it with lower calories so that I can still lose weight."

Let me describe the exact nature of dieting. Dieting allows you to chew and to stay near food. It is a secret relationship with candy hidden in your pocket. Each dieter has their favorite diet foods that they have got in small units with known calories. You are using low-calorie foods so that you can eat more volume. You count calories so that you can control your intake. If you have had your quota, you try to stop. That is a diet.

Disclaimer: Sometimes people eat the same things over and over—for example, peanut butter sandwiches every day. It could look like a diet, but it is not a diet. That is called a routine. It appears that God allows this, for most thin eaters, children, and animals eat this way. If you go to another country, they eat the same things over and over.

However, dieting allows you to have larger volume so that you can be around the food longer or allows you to swallow more, and that is wrong. Do you understand that this has got to go? I am not saying that every food has to be high-calorie; however, if you are cutting back calories so you can eat more volume, then you more than likely are not a routine person but a "dieter."

You need to let go of control, because you will become "out-of-control!" You need to find out what the body is calling for, because in the end, eating the same thing over and over with large volumes of low-calorie foods will extradite a binge. You are asking for your life to be defined by nighttime binge eating or binge eating every two or three days that you cannot control or stop. You will find yourself at one weight, and then in a year or two find yourself heavier, and in another year or two heavier, and then in five years, ten years, heavier. You will lose control, because a "controller" will gain weight. Why? Dieting has no value in restraining your sensual indulgence. People are greedy, and greed grows. The only people who are not greedy are those controlled by God. People-controllers are not controlled by God's Spirit, which is the only Spirit that has control of greed. The only thing that can save mankind is God's Spirit. Man's spirit is greedy by nature. Each year, you will have more and more greed for self. That means that you will want more and more food. That is automatic. Look at America: God has given the greedy people over to their own control. If you do not stop now and get under God's control, you WILL BE OVERWEIGHT IN TIME.

Change this control, and you will automatically become less greedy, and that will automatically result in weight loss. Yeah!

Control is the biggest issue. The controller usually describes who is left in a situation where they cannot lose their weight. They can sometimes have the sweetest personalities in the world, yet underneath they are the most stubborn and controlling people on the planet. They are basically saying to the God of the universe and all men and mankind, spouse, church leaders, everybody, "I am going to control my food, and you are not going to take that one part of my life from me. I am going to control it."

When you fast, it does not need to be about you controlling; it needs to be about surrender. The concept that you continually want to bring up is not "I am going to do this," but it is bringing this issue of idolatry to the table and reminding yourself that this has got to go. "I am choosing a new lifestyle. I am in the committed class, and therefore I am not going back. I cannot keep doing what I was doing, so I have got to make some changes. I have got to be a different person, so I am going to surrender this hour to God. I am going to surrender this desire to eat to God."

When you diet, you are following man-made rules, because they are your rules—even if you have gone in there and tried every diet, and now it is down to your personal diet of eating nuts and wine, or you are eating just M&Ms and rice cakes [whatever your "successful" quick-fix combo of food is]. When you make that choice, you are not committed to this class or God or Christ because you are making the choice to follow man-made rules, and you cannot have it both ways.

God's rule—let us return to the basics—God's rule is for you to wait for the stomach to growl when the body needs it. You are not to be chewing. We have even mentioned the chewing of gum being partially a form of dieting, because you are still with the food; you get to chew. We are getting rid of the chewing action when the stomach is not growling. We can only associate chewing with the stomach growling, because that is what God wants. That will end your controlling lifestyle.

Weigh Down Basics: When you feel an urge to eat and you are not hungry, it is hunger for God! Go to His Word or the tapes or the *BREAKTHROUGH* Workbook. Do not hang out near food. Get it out of your purse, office, desk, and/or car. Do not depend on food. Do not long for the food. Do not look for the food. Pray "God, clean up my mind." Pray, "God, in the name of Jesus Christ, take away this nagging head hunger, this longing, and turn that back into a longing to be inside Your will and to have Your approval. Amen."

The whole concept is that you are changing your lifestyle. Why? Dieting allows you to stay in love with the food. End the diet, and get under "God's control," and you will love God. That is the transfer.

BREAKTHROUGH

Daily Thought Questions

- What has been the biggest revelation that hit your heart this week from the video? This is called a...
   #### BREAKTHROUGH CONVICTION.
   Write these out and collect them over the next eight weeks. Record them each week and rewrite them on the permanent Breakthrough Conviction Chart in the front of the book. You can have several of these convictions per week. Make sure to go over these every week. Even if it seems stupid [that is satan's whisper], write them down. *Example: I am finally realizing that the only way to lose weight is to wait for true hunger each time.*

- Now take this *Breakthrough Conviction* and make a change in your life. When you make a small or big change in your lifestyle from these convictions it is called a...
   #### BREAKTHROUGH LIFESTYLE CHANGE.
   Record them each week and rewrite them on the permanent Breakthrough Lifestyle Change Chart in the front of the book. Praise God for them, and make sure you note the weight lifted off of you because you are changing to obey God rather than Self.

- REPETITION OF SINS MUST STOP. You may not get another chance to get it right. What sin are you repeating, and what have you done today to stop that?

Lesson 2

BLESSINGS FOR OBEDIENCE
❏ Praise God for the Breakthrough!!! Use this space to praise God for what He has done so far. Record these each week and rewrite them on the Blessings for Obedience Chart in the front of the book. How neat that the whole world is wonderful and life is worth living if we just focus on God for the day! *Example: I feel a heavy burden being lifted off my mind and body when I obey God.*

CURSES FOR DISOBEDIENCE
❏ Use this space for the unfortunate times that you take your eyes off of God. [Also rewrite them on the Curses for Disobedience Chart in the front of the book.] I have been at this for years and I have seen that people are quick to forget the problems and curses that are caused by taking their eyes off of God. Make this a frequented page. It will turn you around before you binge.

❏ Did you deny head hunger this week? Did you eat with mouth hunger? Totally analyze your head hunger—with who, what, when, where, how, and why did it happen, and write this down.

Dieting/Control

- What have you been doing to "control" your weight over the last few years? Write out your old pattern in the space provided.

- Write out your new pattern in the space provided below.

- Did you pass your temptation to diet and instead only use your internal stomach hunger to guide you? ❏ Yes ❏ No
- Did you PREPARE to pass your dieting/control test?
  ❏ Yes ❏ No
- What places or foods lead you into temptation to diet?

Greed

- Were you tempted to be greedy with food today? ❏ Yes ❏ No
- Where are you tempted to be greedy? Home? Work?

- Did you pass your test and WAIT for a true stomach growl?
  ❏ Yes ❏ No
- Did you pass your test and stop at full—and God's lead?
  ❏ Yes ❏ No

❏ How did it feel when you controlled your day and your caloric intake? How much time did it eat up?

❏ How does it feel to let go of control? What was your relationship with God like before, and what does it feel like now?

❏ The overeater swallows too much and drinks too much; the hand goes to the mouth too much. Pay attention and see if you are biting your nails, smoking, chewing tobacco, chewing gum or hard candy, drinking, etc. How often is it? Report what you find here. Make a list below of new things for your mind to "chew on." You can even replace your usual spots for gum in your purse, car, etc. with a Pocket Temptation Guide or a favorite Scripture.
   1.
   2.
   3.
   4.
   5.

❏ You may feel like you can wait for the growl but have trouble STOPPING at full. Go back to *The Tablet* book and list how NOT to eat past full.
   1.
   2.
   3.
   4.
   5.

BREAKTHROUGH

Self-Focus

- ❏ How many hours today did you spend on yourself or things for selfish motives/selfish ambition?

- ❏ Did you prepare for having no selfish ambition today?
  ❏ Yes ❏ No
- ❏ Where are the areas in your life that you feel you have selfish ambition, such as…children, work, finances, looks, laziness, material possessions, house, shopping, knowledge, pride, selfish ambition? Any other areas?

- ❏ If you ever feel like you have stumbled, why not pick yourself up and stick to the basics? You cannot waste any time analyzing it or in self-pity. Have you put Bibles and Weigh Down material out around your tempting areas? Fill up your mind with encouragement tapes, sermons, etc., versus lusts for food or self. You cannot lust. Get out of yourself! Are you ready/committed to NOT DIETING tomorrow—Are you ready/set/committed to only using your internal stomach's hunger and fullness to guide you? ❏ Yes ❏ No
- ❏ Write down a testimony of success if you have one from this week. Write down a testimony from someone else in the class who had success this week. [Remember: Send in your before picture!]

LESSON 2

❏ Help keep the focus off of yourself during the day. Pray for someone else. Write out a prayer list for this week:

❏ Have you made a decision to suffer with Christ? Are you committed to have some suffering and a little bit of pain—for better or for worse? ❏ Yes ❏ No

❏ There is a vicious cycle going on from dieting/control to greed to self-focus back to dieting/control. To break this cycle, use the following chart.

	DAYTIME: DIET OR GOD'S LEAD?	AFTERNOON: DIET OR GOD'S LEAD?	NIGHTTIME: DIET OR GOD'S LEAD?	DAYTIME: GREEDY OR SELF-CONTROLLED?	AFTERNOON: GREEDY OR SELF-CONTROLLED?	NIGHTTIME: GREEDY OR SELF-CONTROLLED?
SUNDAY						
MONDAY						
TUESDAY						
WEDNESDAY						
THURSDAY						
FRIDAY						
SATURDAY						

Prayer

Father, we just praise Your holy name, God, for letting us live today. Father, thank You for this opportunity to deny ourselves and to have more of You and less of our own way. Not our will but Yours be done, and therefore You are glorified and giving us this opportunity to have this relationship. Thank You God that You have not forsaken this crowd—any of us. Thank You for this chance. Thank You for this opportunity. Thank You for this very day that we get to deny ourselves and tomorrow, Father. We just praise You because it's so beautiful. I thank You so much for the success of this so far, and help all of those who are discouraged. Comfort them, God. Help them not to go to food for comfort. Help them to see that they can do this and for them to get right back up and eat less, focus less on the food and more on what You want. Help there to be a purging of all idols and a longing for a clinging to You and You alone. We love You God. Thank You for this life and thank You for this class. All this we pray through Jesus' name. Amen.

Answered Prayers

You can break through into this freedom of being connected to God's Spirit, hour by hour, by constant input, then constant praying, and then looking for the answered prayers. Write in your journal your answered prayers from this week.

Stop right now and pray. Pray for someone else. Doing this means you're out of yourself. It's a sign that you are getting back out of self. Out of your self, living for others, living for God. That will be richly blessed.

BREAKTHROUGH

Day: _____

Hour by Hour

Finding the Spirit of God

Hour	Wait for God's lead?	Comments
6:00 AM	☐ Yes ☐ No	
7:00 AM	☐ Yes ☐ No	
8:00 AM	☐ Yes ☐ No	
9:00 AM	☐ Yes ☐ No	
10:00 AM	☐ Yes ☐ No	
11:00 AM	☐ Yes ☐ No	
12:00 PM	☐ Yes ☐ No	
1:00 PM	☐ Yes ☐ No	
2:00 PM	☐ Yes ☐ No	
3:00 PM	☐ Yes ☐ No	
4:00 PM	☐ Yes ☐ No	
5:00 PM	☐ Yes ☐ No	
6:00 PM	☐ Yes ☐ No	
7:00 PM	☐ Yes ☐ No	
8:00 PM	☐ Yes ☐ No	
9:00 PM	☐ Yes ☐ No	
10:00 PM	☐ Yes ☐ No	
11:00 PM	☐ Yes ☐ No	
Middle of the night	☐ Yes ☐ No	

Could you have done a better job today? Explain.

BreakthroughSeries.org   WeighDown.com

BREAKTHROUGH Series

Day: _____

Hour by Hour
Finding the Spirit of God

Hour	Wait for God's lead?	Comments
6:00 AM	☐ Yes ☐ No	
7:00 AM	☐ Yes ☐ No	
8:00 AM	☐ Yes ☐ No	
9:00 AM	☐ Yes ☐ No	
10:00 AM	☐ Yes ☐ No	
11:00 AM	☐ Yes ☐ No	
12:00 PM	☐ Yes ☐ No	
1:00 PM	☐ Yes ☐ No	
2:00 PM	☐ Yes ☐ No	
3:00 PM	☐ Yes ☐ No	
4:00 PM	☐ Yes ☐ No	
5:00 PM	☐ Yes ☐ No	
6:00 PM	☐ Yes ☐ No	
7:00 PM	☐ Yes ☐ No	
8:00 PM	☐ Yes ☐ No	
9:00 PM	☐ Yes ☐ No	
10:00 PM	☐ Yes ☐ No	
11:00 PM	☐ Yes ☐ No	
Middle of the night	☐ Yes ☐ No	

Could you have done a better job today? Explain.

BreakthroughSeries.org   WeighDown.com

Day: _____

BREAKTHROUGH Series

Hour by Hour

Finding the Spirit of God

Hour	Wait for God's lead?	Comments
6:00 AM	☐ Yes ☐ No	
7:00 AM	☐ Yes ☐ No	
8:00 AM	☐ Yes ☐ No	
9:00 AM	☐ Yes ☐ No	
10:00 AM	☐ Yes ☐ No	
11:00 AM	☐ Yes ☐ No	
12:00 PM	☐ Yes ☐ No	
1:00 PM	☐ Yes ☐ No	
2:00 PM	☐ Yes ☐ No	
3:00 PM	☐ Yes ☐ No	
4:00 PM	☐ Yes ☐ No	
5:00 PM	☐ Yes ☐ No	
6:00 PM	☐ Yes ☐ No	
7:00 PM	☐ Yes ☐ No	
8:00 PM	☐ Yes ☐ No	
9:00 PM	☐ Yes ☐ No	
10:00 PM	☐ Yes ☐ No	
11:00 PM	☐ Yes ☐ No	
Middle of the night	☐ Yes ☐ No	

Could you have done a better job today? Explain.

BreakthroughSeries.org   WeighDown.com

BREAKTHROUGH *Series*

Day: _____

Hour by Hour

Finding the Spirit of God

Hour	Wait for God's lead?	Comments
6:00 AM	☐ Yes ☐ No	
7:00 AM	☐ Yes ☐ No	
8:00 AM	☐ Yes ☐ No	
9:00 AM	☐ Yes ☐ No	
10:00 AM	☐ Yes ☐ No	
11:00 AM	☐ Yes ☐ No	
12:00 PM	☐ Yes ☐ No	
1:00 PM	☐ Yes ☐ No	
2:00 PM	☐ Yes ☐ No	
3:00 PM	☐ Yes ☐ No	
4:00 PM	☐ Yes ☐ No	
5:00 PM	☐ Yes ☐ No	
6:00 PM	☐ Yes ☐ No	
7:00 PM	☐ Yes ☐ No	
8:00 PM	☐ Yes ☐ No	
9:00 PM	☐ Yes ☐ No	
10:00 PM	☐ Yes ☐ No	
11:00 PM	☐ Yes ☐ No	
Middle of the night	☐ Yes ☐ No	

Could you have done a better job today? Explain.

BreakthroughSeries.org   WeighDown.com

BREAKTHROUGH Series

Day: _____

HOUR BY HOUR

Finding the Spirit of God

Hour	Wait for God's lead?	Comments
6:00 AM	☐ Yes ☐ No	
7:00 AM	☐ Yes ☐ No	
8:00 AM	☐ Yes ☐ No	
9:00 AM	☐ Yes ☐ No	
10:00 AM	☐ Yes ☐ No	
11:00 AM	☐ Yes ☐ No	
12:00 PM	☐ Yes ☐ No	
1:00 PM	☐ Yes ☐ No	
2:00 PM	☐ Yes ☐ No	
3:00 PM	☐ Yes ☐ No	
4:00 PM	☐ Yes ☐ No	
5:00 PM	☐ Yes ☐ No	
6:00 PM	☐ Yes ☐ No	
7:00 PM	☐ Yes ☐ No	
8:00 PM	☐ Yes ☐ No	
9:00 PM	☐ Yes ☐ No	
10:00 PM	☐ Yes ☐ No	
11:00 PM	☐ Yes ☐ No	
Middle of the night	☐ Yes ☐ No	

Could you have done a better job today? Explain.

BreakthroughSeries.org   WeighDown.com

A Breakthrough Moment
Contrite vs. Controlling

Dear Saints,

From Isaiah 66:2, "This is the one I esteem: he who is humble and contrite in spirit, and trembles at my word."

God loves those who are broken—those who do not want to control Him anymore. The more you have gone down the path of making yourself the center of the universe and the more that you have been spoiled, the harder this death-to-self is. How quickly we can be spoiled. How good it is to take time to look inward and fast and pray, and also pray for others.

The chapter continues in verse 3, "But whoever sacrifices a bull is like one who kills a man, and whoever offers a lamb, like one who breaks a dog's neck; whoever makes a grain offering is like one who presents pig's blood, and whoever burns memorial incense, like one who worships an idol. They have chosen their own ways, and their souls delight in their abominations..."

The "religious sacrificer" is the one who always is "doing things" for the Lord but never "doing what God tells them to do." How angry does it make you when your children, wife, employees, etc., do not do what you say? How much do you like the "make up gift," if it is given to say, " I am never going to do what you want—this gift is all and it's the best you are going to get out of me, so you had better accept it." Reluctant obedience is no fun either. How mad does it make God? Read the following Scriptures from Isaiah 66:

"...so I also will choose harsh treatment for them and will bring upon them what they dread. For when I called, no one answered, when I spoke, no one listened. They did evil in my sight and chose what displeases me...Yet they will be put to shame. Hear that uproar from the city, hear that noise from the temple! It is the sound of the LORD repaying his enemies all they deserve."... the hand of the LORD will be made known to his servants, but his fury will be shown to his foes. See, the LORD is coming with fire, and his chariots are like a whirlwind; he will bring down his anger with fury, and his rebuke with flames of fire. For with fire and with his sword the LORD will execute judgment upon all men, and many will be those slain by the LORD. Those who consecrate and purify themselves to go into the gardens, following the one in the midst of those who eat the flesh of pigs and rats and other abominable things—they will meet their end together," declares the LORD... "As the new heavens and the new earth that I make will endure before me," declares the LORD, "so will your name and descendants endure. From one New Moon to another and from one Sabbath to another, all mankind will come and bow down before me," says the LORD. "And they will go out and look upon the dead bodies of those who rebelled against me; their worm will not die, nor will their fire be quenched, and they will be loathsome to all mankind."

Contrite is rewarded and controlling is punished, rebuked, put to shame, and brought to their end. You cannot be just a little controlling and escape judgment. A little controlling is controlling. You must be a self-less, Godly [Godlike, Christlike], blameless leader or head of household, and then teach your family to be contrite and let go of control.

A servant of God,

Weekly Checklist

- ❑ Read your "Confession & Commitment" page every day
- ❑ Watch Video Three in class
- ❑ Listen to Audio Three
- ❑ Add to your Breakthrough Convictions & Breakthrough Lifestyle Changes Charts
- ❑ Add to your Blessings for Obedience & Curses for Disobedience Charts
- ❑ Make notes in your *BREAKTHROUGH* Journal
- ❑ Answer Week Three Daily Thought Questions
- ❑ Use your Reinforcement Resources & Truth Cards
- ❑ Fill in your Hour By Hour Chart
- ❑ Journal your Answered Prayers
- ❑ As you feel led, fill out the Weight Chart

Reinforcement Resources

- ❑ *Rise Above* — Read Chapter 6 entitled "Secret of the Prison"
- ❑ *Exodus Out of Egypt* — Listen to original Audio 6 entitled "Dodging the Draft"
- ❑ *Weigh Down at Home* — Watch DVD Lessons 2 & 3
- ❑ *Laying Down Your Idols Devotional* — Read June 26th "Obedience = Freedom, Disobedience = Slavery"
- ❑ *Constant Encouragement* — Listen to "Don't Mix the Message" Year 1, Volume 42
- ❑ *The Tablet* — Read Chapter 13 entitled "Love The Lord Your God With All Your Heart"

Scriptures

- ❑ Psalms 36:1-4
- ❑ I Thessalonians 5:1-11
- ❑ Daniel 9:1-17 [Daniel's Prayer]
- ❑ Colossians 2:20-23
- ❑ Mark 4:30-32
- ❑ Psalm 18
- ❑ II Timothy 3:1-5

Lesson Three

A Relationship with God

*I*t is time to make a choice this week to never go back. NO MORE DIETING! You have got to go back to hunger and fullness—the basics. You have one goal every day, and that is to wait for the growl. And then when you do growl, remember that your volume of food should be small, because you are still losing excess weight. Are you not sick to the death of your greed for food? Has it not robbed you of everything? Time, clothing, relationships—food has robbed you of it all. Now is the time to go forward, not backwards. Let us leave this old love of food behind. If you stumble or fall, just pick yourself right back up and wait on the next growl.

Now, if you feel led by God, fasting is a beautiful way to get yourself back on track. When you are overweight, fasting does not hurt at all; but rather, it feels great to relieve your body of all that extra food that makes you so tired. When you have extra weight, fasting is only hard in the mind because of your "head-hunger." But fasting is a great way to experience God providing. Keep saying to yourself, "I don't deserve to go back to my own life of greed. From now on, I'm going to go to GOD when I need help, and I'm going to let Him help me through my emptiness and pain. I'm going to let Him provide an easy way to let go of this food. God, please make the temptation of food go away." God will answer that prayer if He knows you WANT to lay the idol of food down. If you want God more than the food, He will be right there with you to help you. He is GOD—He can make this easy for you. Keep running to Him.

Remember, the battle is all in your mind, and it feels great to fast when you have weight to lose. It also gets easier and easier each hour as you continue. Get a list of all the things you could be doing during this fast...all the drawers you need to clean out, all the cards you need to write, all the rooms you need to clean, all the outfits you need to lay out for the kids, all the people you could encourage. Take it hour by hour—going to God, listening to a tape, going to His Word, singing a song—getting your mind OFF of the food! Say to yourself, "No more of that old life centered around food! I'm ready for a NEW life!"

Now, think further to the next generation. It's time to pass a new life down to your children—not one that is focused on food, but rather, a life that is totally FOCUSED on God alone and doing His will hour by hour. Keep all of your motives for doing this hour by hour for GOD—and for the NEXT GENERATION! This is exciting! You should be excited to find this answer, for if you continue to go growl to growl with small portions of food, then you WILL lose the extra weight!

The main thing to focus on is OBEDIENCE TO GOD with hunger and fullness. When you are tempted to overeat, remember that eating too much wears you out. It robs you of your time, your finances, your relationships, your self-esteem—and puts a wedge between you and your spouse. This food has not been a good "god" or a good friend at all. It has made you its slave, and it has demanded that you bow down to it all the time. You have been a SLAVE to the food, and it has made you empty. Notice that you are still looking for a feeling to fill you up even after you have overeaten. But when you are tempted, just go into your room, get on your knees and pray, "O God, please help me pass this test. Help me to see that I CAN do this, and help me to set a great example for others. Help me to prove it to myself that I love You more than that food. Help me through this hour of testing. Please, O God, deliver me from this temptation and show me the Kingdom work You have planned for me to do tonight instead." Then as you pray that, God will allow you to get distracted through those tempting hours, and you will look up and you will have made it through the nighttime hours! You will get to wake up the next morning and start your day over right and you will be so happy that you passed through your test!

Remember, one huge "NO-NO" is getting up in the middle of the night to eat. You have made it through the day with being aware of what you are doing...but in the night, you must not get distracted, lose focus and run to the food. [Read Psalm 36. "Even on his bed he plots evil..."] And do not fast just to be the one "in control" again. The "controller" can never lose their weight. They may have a sweet personality, but underneath they are so stubborn. They are saying even to the God of the Universe and to everyone else on earth, "I am going to control my food—and you are NOT going to take that away from me." So, if or when you fast, it cannot be about you controlling. It must be about you SURRENDERING to God. It must be about laying this idol of food down. It is all about laying this love and greed for food down—and gaining a relationship with God!

Keep reminding yourself: "I am NOT going back to control and overeating...I've got to make some serious, lifetime changes. I've got to be a different person. I'm going to surrender these hours over to GOD and doing His will." Remember, dieting and saying, "yes" to dieting is very possibly you saying, "I'm not going to let go of the food. I am not committed. I am going to maneuver around idolatry. I'm going to stay with the food and chewing more and I'm going to eat foods with fewer calories so that I can chew more." Dieting allows you to count calories or keep little foods or candies with you at all times. It allows you to think about the food more often and eat a greater volume of food.

Eating your same favorite foods over and over is not necessarily dieting. Dieting is when you are eating certain foods so that you can eat again later, or whenever you want to. You are never letting go of control. You are staying in control of when you eat and what you eat. You are still being the "god" of your eating, and The True God is not a part of your plan. You are not looking for God's lead with dieting—you are looking to your own lead. Dieting and staying around the food all the time must go. You will never lose the love of food unless you stop dieting and let go of control. If you are in control of your eating and you just eat the same low-calorie foods over and over and over, you are just asking for a temptation to binge later. It makes you want to binge when you've forced yourself to eat the same foods over and over and over. It makes you want to binge when you've dieted and kept the food around all day long, never getting your mind OFF the food. Diets simply cause binges. Your life will be bound to binge eating every few nights with dieting, and with each passing year, your binges will make you get larger and larger and larger.

Diets will never make you self-controlled—they make you get OUT of control. Man-made rules [or diets] will never sanctify you or give you the self-control you desire. But in contrast, self-control comes from obedience to God. Only in obeying the commands of God do you receive FREEDOM from food and self-control. That's why the 10 Commandments—the Tablets—are so PRICELESS. They are the commands that came straight from God. They are commands that sanctify. Go back to the basics of Weigh Down and read the Scripture [Colossians 2:20] that steers you away from man-made rules, such as dieting. Man-made rules lack ANY value in restraining sensual indulgence!!

You only have one thing to concentrate on, you only have one thing to do, and that is to concentrate on your relationship with God.

This is all about a relationship with God. A controlling person has a relationship with themselves. They know every detail about themselves, and their mind is constantly returning to thinking about what they need. Their mouths and conversations will invariably return to talking about themselves and their wants, their needs, their desires. With each passing year, the dieter is more in love with the food and less in love with God. The relationship with God cannot proceed until the control is laid down. The control leads to dieting, which leads to greed, and the greed leads to being out of control.

It is all about walking with God. When you look for men who have been lifted up by God—Abraham, Moses, David, the Apostle Paul, and especially the Son of God, Jesus Christ—all have a common denominator: they walked with God. God's Spirit led them. They prayed about their hour and their upcoming hours. They worried, I am sure, if they were walking in the Spirit. Paul will talk about the Spirit leading him and then later blocking him from going places. Many Prophets talk about the Spirit "taking them" somewhere. When you look back on your life, you can see that by the grace of God, and unconsciously, you have been moved and led by God. Praise Him for doing more for you than you could think or ask. One of the best proof-texts that God is leading you so that you might find Him is found in Acts 17:24-28:

> "The God who made the world and everything in it is the Lord of heaven and earth and does not live in temples built by hands. And he is not served by human hands, as if he needed anything, because he himself gives all men life and breath and everything else. From one man he made every nation of men, that they should inhabit the whole earth; and he determined the times set for them and the exact places where they should live. God did this so that men would seek him and perhaps reach out for him and find him, though he is not far from each one of us. 'For in him we live and move and have our being.' As some of your own poets have said, 'We are his offspring.'"

What if this is right? What if the only thing in the world that matters is your personal relationship with God and Christ? This entails leaving the love of the world, and it entails embracing suffering as well as the blessings. Paul threw everything into knowing Jesus Christ and sharing in His sufferings. This suffering changes your life. If you are always preventing suffering, then you are spoiled and you do not understand Christ and therefore mere Christianity. Christ suffered, and His example is to be followed. Read I Peter 2 and Hebrews 5. Do not rob yourself or your children of suffering for Christ. Waiting for hunger is wrapped up in embracing suffering. Why deny yourself of suffering that will only bring you good in the end? Think about suffering — it is short lived and you do not remember it, but you keep the product of the suffering forever. Some will wait for a day or a week for hunger, but what they have not embraced is the DAILY cross. The "come and go" Christian is the most miserable, for they are neither fully in nor out. That is why their relationship with God and Christ suffers. But if you will follow Christ, you will find the relationship with God. Christ embraced DAILY suffering for God and yet experienced DAILY JOY and a powerful relationship with God. Choose Christ as your Lord today and follow Him! But don't make this choice for just one or two weeks. The average person can prepare themselves to suffer for the first one or two or even three weeks of classes, but you must make a conscious choice to embrace suffering as a way of life. Do this, and it will make all the difference!

Relationship with God

Believe it or not, your relationship with God is connected to your weight. The average person has a tendency to feel very secure with their relationship with God. Some of the latest surveys in America show that up to 90% of the population believe that God is pleased with them and that they are going to Heaven. From the early part of

> You yourselves have seen what I did to Egypt, and how I carried you on eagles' wings and brought you to myself.
>
> Exodus 19:4

this century all the way to the 1980s, the average Christian, which is the predominant religion in America, believed that trust and belief in Christ was necessary to enter Heaven. However, now many believe that Heaven is open to atheists as well as believers. All this says is that the lie that Christ relaxed our response to God has taken root and gone to a new level. The truth is that love poured from the Heavens needs to be met with love in return.

We need a respectful, well thought-out response to the opportunity offered us by the Heavens. Grace should not give us a license to sin, but rather it should make us grateful that we even have a chance in a lifetime to enter the race to the finish line. Think about it! We could just be a bystander watching others respond to the love of the Father. We have a chance to win God's favor—to get close to God. Do not waste this opportunity. The closer you get to God, the more you will drop the love of food. Now let us tell the truth of where we are so that we can see how much further we have to go.

Survey

❑ Please describe your relationship with God as best as you can:

❑ How many times did you pray today?
Where were you when you prayed?
Do you ever pray on your knees?
If yes, how often?
How many answered prayers did you have today?
This week?
This month?

BREAKTHROUGH

- ❏ In the last 3 months, how many times did you turn to God or His Word during a temptation?

- ❏ How often do you turn to the truth by either listening to a tape, reading God's Word, or focusing on workbooks or homework?
  ❏ Never ❏ Weekly ❏ Two times per week ❏ Daily

- ❏ When are your problem hours with eating?

- ❏ How much do you love food and eating now?

- ❏ When was the last time that you were able to really have a Breakthrough and lose a significant amount of weight or greed with food?

- ❏ How much stronger is the pull for food now compared to what it was in the past?

- ❏ Do you ever forget to turn to God for help?

- ❏ Do you sometimes forget that God and Christ are by your side or right in the room with you?

Lesson 3

- ❏ What words best describe how you feel about your relationship with God and Christ right now? [For example: strong, weak, erratic, etc.]

- ❏ Do you ever feel God-forsaken? ❏ Yes ❏ No
  Explain:

- ❏ Read Ephesians 4:17-19. Have you ever felt "given over" as described in Ephesians 4? Write out these verses here:

- ❏ Read Ezekiel 18. Do you know that there is hope for those who repent?

- ❏ Write out the following Scriptures:
  - Ezekiel 18:31-32

  - Isaiah 59:20

- Acts 2:38

- Acts 3:19

❑ Do you describe yourself as a binge eater? If so, how often does this happen?

❑ Do you ever get up in the night and eat?

❑ Have you had closer moments with God in the past than you do now? Describe:

❑ How important do you think a relationship with God is, and how connected to salvation is it? Read Matthew 7:21.

❑ Name some people you think are close to God. How is your life different?

LESSON 3

❑ Name or list all of your jobs, activities, hobbies, and interests. How many "hats" do you wear?

❑ What do you think is getting in your way of having a better relationship with God? What could you say "No" to?

❑ What should you be doing to protect this relationship with God? A correct relationship with God will end your relationship with the food.

DAILY THOUGHT QUESTIONS

- What has been the biggest revelation that hit your heart this week from the video? This is called a...
  ### BREAKTHROUGH CONVICTION.
  Write these out and collect them over the next eight weeks. Record them each week and rewrite them on the permanent Breakthrough Conviction Chart in the front of the book. You can have several of these convictions per week. Make sure to go over these every week. Even if it seems stupid [that is satan's whisper], write them down. *Example: I am finally realizing that the only way to lose weight is to wait for true hunger each time.*

- Now take this *Breakthrough Conviction* and make a change in your life. When you make a small or big change in your lifestyle from these convictions it is called a...
  ### BREAKTHROUGH LIFESTYLE CHANGE.
  Record them each week and rewrite them on the permanent Breakthrough Lifestyle Change Chart in the front of the book. Praise God for them and make sure you note the weight lifted off of you because you are changing to obey God rather than Self.

- REPETITION OF SINS MUST STOP. You may not get another chance to get it right. What sin are you repeating, and what have you done today to stop that?

BLESSINGS FOR OBEDIENCE

❏ Praise God for the Breakthrough!!! Use this space to praise God for what He has done so far. Record these each week and rewrite them on the Blessings for Obedience Chart in the front of the book. How neat that the whole world is wonderful and life is worth living if we just focus on God for the day! *Example: I feel a heavy burden being lifted off my mind and body when I obey God.*

CURSES FOR DISOBEDIENCE

❏ Use this space for the unfortunate times that you take your eyes off of God. [Also rewrite them on the Curses for Disobedience Chart in the front of the book.] I have been at this for years, and I have seen that people are quick to forget the problems and curses that are caused by taking their eyes off of God. Make this a frequented page. It will turn you around before you binge.

❏ Did you deny head hunger this week? Did you eat with mouth hunger? Totally analyze your head hunger—with who, what, when, where, how, and why did it happen and write this down.

❏ When you are learning to walk, you might stumble, but eventually you will fly like the eagle. Always repent, confess, pray, and start over quickly if you have messed up. People usually reason that, "I've blown it," and so they wait for days before they start over. This is no longer an option. If you stumble over the next 8 weeks, turn to this page and record your victorious and successful WAIT for the next true stomach hunger.

Stumble Date:

Successfully waited for the growl?
Length of time you waited:

Unsuccessfully waited for the growl?
Length of time you waited:

❏ God will be testing to see if your commitment is real. Give every growl to God. Get ready every day for every test. If your temptation is in the late evening and the growl has not come around, please go do something else. Visit or take care of your friends, your children or your spouse. What about cleaning out a drawer in the house every evening or finishing that photo album? Please do not eat. Take yourself away from that kitchen. Write down the situations or temptations you are going to avoid this week and how you will avoid them.

- ❏ Does the scale dictate your mood? Write do

- ❏ You cannot open the door to self-pity anymore. Can you think of a time when you went into this type of downward spiral? What will you do differently next time?

- ❏ Contrast how you feel when you obey vs. when you are in sin:

- ❏ What audios are you listening to this week?

- ❏ What praise songs or other music have helped you keep your focus on God? [Write out the verses of the song that really helped you.]

Read Isaiah Chapter 6. What do you do when you receive correction?

- ❑ If you ever feel like you are losing focus, you always need to go back to the basics. List the basics here:

- ❑ Did you feel any struggle this week? Write it out:

- ❑ Now write out how you overcame that struggle so that you can remember.

- ❑ When you started this class, how long did you wait for the first growl?

LESSON 3

❑ Some wait hours for stomach hunger, while others might wait for days. Write down what true hunger feels like so that you can distinguish it from head hunger.
<u>*Stomach Hunger:*</u>   <u>*Head Hunger:*</u>

Remember: When a thin eater is really hungry, they know exactly what they want, but if they are not hungry, they cannot tell what foods really sound good. Hunger to an overweight person is slight compared to someone who has already lost their excess weight.

❑ After a lifetime of thin eating, how does a thin eater view food? *Note: You may want to find a thin eater this week and ask them.*

❑ Why is this class working for you? How is your commitment different this time around? [Copy this commitment down on a card and carry it around with you to help keep your focus.]

❑ Remember: making a true confession to this greed for more food is what got you started in this class. Re-write your confession and the conviction you felt from making that confession in Week One. Have you kept that conviction?

LESSON 3

Prayer

O Father, we love you so much. You are an incredible Creator and an incredible Lord of Lords and King of Kings, an incredible God, and now such a gentle God in directing us and disciplining us and teaching us the way to go. Thank you for not abandoning us. Thank you, Father, for helping us to see your words and what to obey. Thank you for your Spirit, which is the only Spirit that has self-control. Thank you for blessing this class. With the stock market dropping and everything going out of control and people being very afraid, we are grounded on a Rock of Jesus Christ and obedience and commitment to You and You alone. Thank you for the blessings that come along with it. Thank you that we can be free from idols.

God, I pray that you will guide us and lead us. Father, I want to thank you for this beautiful class that is becoming more and more like Christ every week. Thank you for their committed hearts. May the energy in this class grow. May it be unlike any other class where people stop coming or they give up in the fourth week or fifth week. May this be the type of class that grows like the tiny mustard seed into a big tree. Father, may we turn into something that draws the world, Father, a class that wants to be committed to You and You alone. We are committed to You, God; we are going away from the food and never returning to it. We are learning every week what to do more and more to get away from that food and onto the food of doing your will. For all this, we praise You in Jesus' name. Amen.

Answered Prayers

You can break through into this freedom of being connected to God's Spirit, hour by hour, by constant input, then constant praying, and then looking for the answered prayers. Write in your journal your answered prayers from this week.

BREAKTHROUGH Series

Day: _____

Hour by Hour

Finding the Spirit of God

Hour	Wait for God's lead?	Comments
6:00 AM	☐ Yes ☐ No	
7:00 AM	☐ Yes ☐ No	
8:00 AM	☐ Yes ☐ No	
9:00 AM	☐ Yes ☐ No	
10:00 AM	☐ Yes ☐ No	
11:00 AM	☐ Yes ☐ No	
12:00 PM	☐ Yes ☐ No	
1:00 PM	☐ Yes ☐ No	
2:00 PM	☐ Yes ☐ No	
3:00 PM	☐ Yes ☐ No	
4:00 PM	☐ Yes ☐ No	
5:00 PM	☐ Yes ☐ No	
6:00 PM	☐ Yes ☐ No	
7:00 PM	☐ Yes ☐ No	
8:00 PM	☐ Yes ☐ No	
9:00 PM	☐ Yes ☐ No	
10:00 PM	☐ Yes ☐ No	
11:00 PM	☐ Yes ☐ No	
Middle of the night	☐ Yes ☐ No	

Could you have done a better job today? Explain.

BreakthroughSeries.org

WeighDown.com

Day: _____

BREAKTHROUGH Series

HOUR BY HOUR

Finding the Spirit of God

Hour	Wait for God's lead?	Comments
6:00 AM	☐ Yes ☐ No	
7:00 AM	☐ Yes ☐ No	
8:00 AM	☐ Yes ☐ No	
9:00 AM	☐ Yes ☐ No	
10:00 AM	☐ Yes ☐ No	
11:00 AM	☐ Yes ☐ No	
12:00 PM	☐ Yes ☐ No	
1:00 PM	☐ Yes ☐ No	
2:00 PM	☐ Yes ☐ No	
3:00 PM	☐ Yes ☐ No	
4:00 PM	☐ Yes ☐ No	
5:00 PM	☐ Yes ☐ No	
6:00 PM	☐ Yes ☐ No	
7:00 PM	☐ Yes ☐ No	
8:00 PM	☐ Yes ☐ No	
9:00 PM	☐ Yes ☐ No	
10:00 PM	☐ Yes ☐ No	
11:00 PM	☐ Yes ☐ No	
Middle of the night	☐ Yes ☐ No	

Could you have done a better job today? Explain.

BreakthroughSeries.org   WeighDown.com

BREAKTHROUGH Series

Day: _____

Hour by Hour
Finding the Spirit of God

Hour	Wait for God's lead?	Comments
6:00 AM	☐ Yes ☐ No	
7:00 AM	☐ Yes ☐ No	
8:00 AM	☐ Yes ☐ No	
9:00 AM	☐ Yes ☐ No	
10:00 AM	☐ Yes ☐ No	
11:00 AM	☐ Yes ☐ No	
12:00 PM	☐ Yes ☐ No	
1:00 PM	☐ Yes ☐ No	
2:00 PM	☐ Yes ☐ No	
3:00 PM	☐ Yes ☐ No	
4:00 PM	☐ Yes ☐ No	
5:00 PM	☐ Yes ☐ No	
6:00 PM	☐ Yes ☐ No	
7:00 PM	☐ Yes ☐ No	
8:00 PM	☐ Yes ☐ No	
9:00 PM	☐ Yes ☐ No	
10:00 PM	☐ Yes ☐ No	
11:00 PM	☐ Yes ☐ No	
Middle of the night	☐ Yes ☐ No	

Could you have done a better job today? Explain.

BreakthroughSeries.org   WeighDown.com

BREAKTHROUGH *Series*

Day: _____

Hour by Hour

Finding the Spirit of God

Hour	Wait for God's lead?	Comments
6:00 AM	☐ Yes ☐ No	
7:00 AM	☐ Yes ☐ No	
8:00 AM	☐ Yes ☐ No	
9:00 AM	☐ Yes ☐ No	
10:00 AM	☐ Yes ☐ No	
11:00 AM	☐ Yes ☐ No	
12:00 PM	☐ Yes ☐ No	
1:00 PM	☐ Yes ☐ No	
2:00 PM	☐ Yes ☐ No	
3:00 PM	☐ Yes ☐ No	
4:00 PM	☐ Yes ☐ No	
5:00 PM	☐ Yes ☐ No	
6:00 PM	☐ Yes ☐ No	
7:00 PM	☐ Yes ☐ No	
8:00 PM	☐ Yes ☐ No	
9:00 PM	☐ Yes ☐ No	
10:00 PM	☐ Yes ☐ No	
11:00 PM	☐ Yes ☐ No	
Middle of the night	☐ Yes ☐ No	

Could you have done a better job today? Explain.

BreakthroughSeries.org   WeighDown.com

BREAKTHROUGH Series

Day: _____

Hour by Hour

Finding the Spirit of God

Hour	Wait for God's lead?	Comments
6:00 AM	☐ Yes ☐ No	
7:00 AM	☐ Yes ☐ No	
8:00 AM	☐ Yes ☐ No	
9:00 AM	☐ Yes ☐ No	
10:00 AM	☐ Yes ☐ No	
11:00 AM	☐ Yes ☐ No	
12:00 PM	☐ Yes ☐ No	
1:00 PM	☐ Yes ☐ No	
2:00 PM	☐ Yes ☐ No	
3:00 PM	☐ Yes ☐ No	
4:00 PM	☐ Yes ☐ No	
5:00 PM	☐ Yes ☐ No	
6:00 PM	☐ Yes ☐ No	
7:00 PM	☐ Yes ☐ No	
8:00 PM	☐ Yes ☐ No	
9:00 PM	☐ Yes ☐ No	
10:00 PM	☐ Yes ☐ No	
11:00 PM	☐ Yes ☐ No	
Middle of the night	☐ Yes ☐ No	

Could you have done a better job today? Explain.

BreakthroughSeries.org   WeighDown.com

LESSON 3

LIKE AN EAGLE SWOOPING DOWN

Remember that we must end the repetition of sin. There are two types of references to eagles in the Bible. One is an eagle that represents God, and the other is a revengeful eagle that is used for destruction on the disobedient. We need to pray for this nation, pray for the church, and pray for ourselves—that we do not rouse God's anger and that His anger turns away from destruction. Take time today to read Deuteronomy 28.

The Lord will bring a nation against you from far away, from the ends of the earth, like an eagle swooping down, a nation whose language you do not understand...

Deuteronomy 28:49

Breakthrough Moment
Walking with God

Dear Seekers,

Are you seeking this peace and joy through a relationship with God and Christ or are you seeking selfish gain and glory?

The Key is to stay near. My puppy dog does not leave my side. When I am sleeping on the bed, she is at my feet. When I get up, she follows me from room to room. She will lie down and sleep in each spot until she hears my feet move. Then she follows me again. She must be sleeping with one eye open. She has several spots where she can get even closer to me, and when I am writing she wants on my lap. She is relentless until she gets closer to me. She greets me at the door every day. She knows my routine. Her focus is on me, and when I am not there or too busy it is on David. She turns circles for David when he comes home. I would not want her around if she did not obey. She obeys better than any dog we have ever had. When I say, "back," she gets back. The point is that she is obviously living for our attention and love, and that is it. She has no greater goal.

Are you that focused on God and getting His love and approval? Are you near God and Christ? Do you watch the feet of Jesus and concentrate on what He did? He always spoke the truth in love and stayed busy in Kingdom work every day, not caring about what naysayers thought but only what the needs of the people were. Christ lost Himself in God and now has right-hand recognition and position and power. Simply put, He has a lot of money, and He will live forever and ever, ruling with God. Is there a higher reward?

Tell me what pays greater dividends. People work out and get exercise and go to the doctor for health check-ups and take a lot of the medicines prescribed to lower blood pressure and prolong life. Nothing lowers your blood pressure more than a relationship with God where you can pray about every worry. Health is from a relationship with the Creator.

Ultimately, it was the transfer of a relationship with the food

LESSON 3

over to a relationship with God that stopped your greed, which resulted in weight loss. Ultimately, it was a relationship with God that gave you more confidence that someone really loved you so that you could love your spouse back. This security resulted in not trying to prove that you were right or to argue, so now your marriage is rewardingly strong. You have no fear of divorce or your love leaving your side. God gets the credit!

You will never lose weight with dieting. Dieting does nothing but increase your relationship with yourself. You will only lose weight with a relationship with God, through hunger and fullness... So make the right choice.

I could go on and on, but you get the picture. Your relationship with God is what you need to concentrate on. Stay near; hold His Word near and dear to your heart; follow His lead. Stay close at hand for whatever is needed to be done. Listen to His voice and obey. Have only eyes and ears and passion for God. Find out what is blocking this relationship and demolish it while you have a chance.

Your friend and servant,

Gwen

Weekly Checklist

- ❑ Read your "Confession & Commitment" page every day
- ❑ Watch Video Four in class
- ❑ Listen to Audio Four
- ❑ Add to your Breakthrough Convictions & Breakthrough Lifestyle Changes Charts
- ❑ Add to your Blessings for Obedience & Curses for Disobedience Charts
- ❑ Make notes in your *BREAKTHROUGH* Journal
- ❑ Answer Week Four Daily Thought Questions
- ❑ Use your Reinforcement Resources & Truth Cards
- ❑ Fill in your Hour By Hour Chart
- ❑ Journal your Answered Prayers
- ❑ As you feel led, fill out the Weight Chart

Reinforcement Resources

- ❑ *Rise Above*—Read Chapter 11 entitled "Estranged from God"
- ❑ *Weigh Down at Home Pocket Temptation Guide*—Find the temptation that you most related to this week and memorize the Scripture for encouragement
- ❑ *Laying Down Your Idols Devotional*—Read November 27th "Choose Today"
- ❑ *Constant Encouragement*—Listen to "Backsliding" Year 1, Volume 16
- ❑ *Constant Encouragement*—Listen to "Blessings vs. Curses" Year 2, Volume 13
- ❑ *The Tablet*—Read Chapter 14 entitled "How To Get The Spirit Of God"

Scriptures

- ❑ Galatians 5:7-9
- ❑ Galatians 5:16-26
- ❑ II Corinthians 5:11-21
- ❑ Romans 8:5
- ❑ Isaiah 40:28-31
- ❑ I Peter 3

Lesson Four

Using Your Power vs. God's Power

*H*ere we are at Week Four. This is the most exciting class on the face of the earth. The reason why is that we are bringing the ancient teaching of commitment back into the forefront of our lives. What are we committed to? We have all repented and confessed that we have chosen the wrong thing to be committed to and have now made a choice to completely commit our lives, soul, heart, mind, and strength to God alone. To commit to God, you have to let go of control of your eating, spending, lusting, talking, bad habits, jealousy, laziness, etc.

People do not realize that they are controlling. Did you wait for hunger—true hunger—every time you ate these past few weeks? When you have been stuck for years and years in any stronghold, your defining characteristic is that you are a controller. Even if you are a sweet one, you are a controller. You have found little ways to look like you are allowing God to lead you, but in reality you are controlling God and spouse and co-workers and children, etc.

Dieting is the opposite of letting go of control. Dieting is a means of controlling your life and bypassing the will of God. That is profound. The whole concept behind this class in a nutshell is to let go of control and let God lead us. Yet there is something inside of man that wants to control. They want to control the people around them, the environment around them.

God is allowing the financial markets to spiral downward, and He is bringing down age-old trusted banks and market institutions. Most people's emotions range from panic and depression to suicide. These emotions reveal that money has become an all-encompassing god. The idolatry is rampant. How immoral is this nation? Very. How do you know? The minute that we hit a recession, theft and white-collar crime and embezzlement are rampant. A controller is basically an immoral, faithless person. Why do controlling people love money? The reason is that this money is a means of control. Money hoarders are worried that they would not be able to call their shots for the rest of their lives—their destiny. They wrongly theorize that with money a person can maintain a lifestyle of choice. Right now, due to high rolling ponzi games, billionaires are finding themselves penniless. When you lose it you do not know if you are going to be sweeping a broom as a janitor. You do not know what you will be doing or what time you will get up. You do not know what is going to be happening.

The same is true for letting go of the control of food. If you have really joined this class—because you can be sitting in this class but you have never really joined in with the class—this class is about being committed. The class is about being committed to God ruling and you letting go of control. If you really mean it, then you do not know where you are going to be today and tomorrow and the next day. You don't know where you're going to be eating, who you are going to be eating with, what you're going to be eating or if you are going to be eating. You have let go of something that has become a god to you. How do I know that food has become a god to you? It is because it has been so difficult to lay it down. What has the food become to you? It has become entertainment, comfort, and the aid to prevent boredom. It has become everything to you.

What is the purpose of this class? It is mere Christianity. You are transferring over the food god to THE GOD so that God is becoming your entertainment. God is your comfort. God is the fun and the joy. When you are tired, you run to God.

If you have struggled with your eating, it is usually because you have become too busy. Under pressure, unprepared sojourners in Christ default and go backwards to their old habits and their old comforts to meet their needs. You feel tired, so you start eating that food. In your mind, the lie that you have grown to embrace is that you feel better when you eat. The truth is that you feel worse when you eat. You feel lethargic, and you can't get as much work done. You're at the end of the day and you feel a little bad about what you've accomplished that day, but you can't put your finger on why. You don't know why you're so tired at 5 o'clock or whenever it is.

The default to your old habits because you are so "busy" puts you back into the driver's seat, and there you are again controlling your day and controlling your eating. You've always made bad decisions. You are a bad god. You are a bad boss of your body. You are a bad ruler. You've messed up.

Paul says in Galatians 5:7-9, "You were running a good race. Who cut in on you and kept you from obeying the truth? That kind of persuasion does not come from the one who calls you. A little yeast works through the whole batch of dough."

You were running a good race these first four weeks, and you were letting go of control. Who threw you into confusion to where you have taken over control? He goes on to say that this person will pay a grave penalty for throwing you into confusion. Nevertheless, you have got to go back, he says in the fifth chapter, and walk in the Spirit. The whole masterful genius key of salvation is walking in the Spirit, finding the Spirit and walking in the Spirit. Therefore you are that person who is listening, sensitive, and back into worrying about missing God and praying constantly for God to guide you—especially around the times that you know you have now fallen into a bad situation where you are doing things yourself and controlling.

You have heard that Jesus came to save us from our sins and set the captives free. Yes, it is the year of the Lord's favor to preach good news to the poor, to bind up the brokenhearted, to proclaim freedom for the captives and release from darkness for the prisoners. This is not as the false churches have led you to believe. It is not to forgive someone who chooses to continue in sin. Jesus came to earth to forgive us of our sins so that we would—as he told the woman caught in adultery—go and sin no more. Being held captive to sin is not good news nor is it favor from God—it is horrifying, for it brings on curses. Favor, and therefore blessings and answered prayers are the result of laying down sin.

Part of the problem of being a controller is that you try to lay down sin with your own methods. What if we have "played god" on freedom from sin and come up with our one counterfeit way to lay down sin? We lay down sin with sin? We lay down sin with sinful solutions? No wonder we struggle with the last pounds, the last drinking, the last lusts, the last pride or greed! We have tried to overcome sin with our power, using sin, vs. using God's power and His Spirit. How clever of satan.

Today is the year of God's favor. Jesus has been revealed to us and He was sinless and overcame by the Holy Spirit of God and cast out demons with the Holy Spirit of God. This is the year of the Breakthrough for those who have used their own strength. You are exhausted and have gotten nowhere.

WHATEVER YOU ARE CONTROLLING IN YOUR LIFE, YOU'VE GOT TO LET GO!

There is only one answer—be born again of a new Spirit. Get rid of your old ways, such as using your power, smarts and strength to diet or manipulate things. Kill that spirit and open up to the power of obeying the Holy Spirit of God. It has no greed for self, but it is the happiest person alive. It is the Spirit that moves all life and angels and the entire Heavenly Kingdom.

We are a group that is most excited and happy because we are not going backwards; we are committed to following only God. We are not going back to the old lifestyle of controlling our day, especially in the area of food or whatever you have signed up for this class for. Whatever is your controlling area, you've got to let it go. You've got to be convinced that you make bad decisions, that you are a bad decision maker, that you cannot rule your life and that your desires and God's desires are in conflict with each other. God's power is better than your power. LET GO AND LET GOD LEAD!

*Put the trumpet to your lips!
An eagle is over the house of the Lord
because the people have broken the covenant
and rebelled against my law.*   Hosea 8:1

BREAKTHROUGH Series

Daily Thought Questions

❑ What has been the biggest revelation that hit your heart this week from the video? This is called a...
   BREAKTHROUGH CONVICTION.
Write these out and collect them over the next eight weeks. Record them each week and rewrite them on the permanent Breakthrough Conviction Chart in the front of the book. You can have several of these convictions per week. Make sure to go over these every week. Even if it seems stupid [that is satan's whisper], write them down. *Example: I am finally realizing that the only way to lose weight is to wait for true hunger each time.*

❑ Now take this *Breakthrough Conviction* and make a change in your life. When you make a small or big change in your lifestyle from these convictions it is called a...
   BREAKTHROUGH LIFESTYLE CHANGE.
Record them each week and rewrite them on the permanent Breakthrough Lifestyle Change Chart in the front of the book. Praise God for them and make sure you note the weight lifted off of you because you are changing to obey God rather than Self.

❑ REPETITION OF SINS MUST STOP. You may not get another chance to get it right. What sin are you repeating, and what have you done today to stop that?

BLESSINGS FOR OBEDIENCE

❑ Praise God for the Breakthrough!!! Use this space to praise God for what He has done so far. Record these each week and rewrite them on the Blessings for Obedience Chart in the front of the book. How neat that the whole world is wonderful and life is worth living if we just focus on God for the day! *Example: I feel a heavy burden being lifted off my mind and body when I obey God.*

CURSES FOR DISOBEDIENCE

❑ Use this space for the unfortunate times that you take your eyes off of God. [Also rewrite them on the Curses for Disobedience Chart in the front of the book.] I have been at this for years, and I have seen that people are quick to forget the problems and curses that are caused by taking their eyes off of God. Make this a frequented page. It will turn you around before you binge.

❑ Did you deny head hunger this week? Did you eat with mouth hunger? Totally analyze your head hunger—with who, what, when, where, how, and why did it happen, and write this down.

BREAKTHROUGH

- ❑ According to the video, if you are a dieter or if you have been struggling and are stuck in a stronghold, what does it really say about you?

- ❑ Do you consider yourself a controller? Explain in detail.

- ❑ Beginning when you wake up and throughout a 24-hour day, what are the ways you have been controlling your day rather than allowing God to control it?

- ❑ God can lead you where to sit at church and how long to stay afterwards. He can lead you to talk to someone at the grocery store. Pray hour by hour, and write down how God leads you that hour.

LESSON 4

- Beware of busyness, because we default to our old controlling habits. What busy events or times are coming up today, this week and this month? What is your plan to slow down and stay committed to God?

- Did you keep a food log? ❑ Yes ❑ No
- Did you pray before you ate? ❑ Yes ❑ No
- Did you read your 7 points? ❑ Yes ❑ No
- Did you wait for your stomach to growl? ❑ Yes ❑ No
- Did you listen to what your body needs? ❑ Yes ❑ No

- Write out Romans 8:5 and memorize it.

- Write out the seven-point list before you eat today and see if it helps you.

BREAKTHROUGH

❑ Does waiting on God and following the Holy Spirit sound boring or too slow to you? Write out a reminder for yourself of the pain that you feel when you don't wait on God, and contrast it to the blessings you have received when you did wait on the Holy Spirit.

❑ Remember the rewards when you follow God's Spirit and write them down [i.e. clothes fit, compliments].

❑ Think back and write down how long you've been controlling the food. Include any plateaus in weight loss. Write down the reasons why you are breaking through and why you are no longer going to plateau anymore at an undesirable weight.

❑ This week, stay focused on Ephesians 5:5. Write it out here:

❏ After this lesson, write out the definitions of these words as you understand them now:

• an immoral person:

• a greedy person:

• impure:

• laying down sin:

❏ You were so forgiven under a counterfeit religious system that it is hard to identify with putting yourself in a sinful category. Are you tired of never really being set free all the way? What are some of the lies you listened to that kept you from feeling conviction from the Holy Spirit? Example: "You're a pretty good person."

❏ If you are struggling with letting go of control, it is because you have so little faith in God's Spirit for your day. When you are giving up and dying to your will, you sometimes forget that something is better on the other side. This forgetfulness is a lack of faith. You must believe in a good God. You must learn to let go of control and get out of God's way. God is in the room and with you everywhere. You must not talk over His Holy Spirit, nor talk back to His Holy Spirit. It comes through authority if you let it. Scripture says to ask for faith and believe. Do not be double-minded or tossed by the wind. Wait on God and build that faith. Without this faith, you cannot please God. Ask for it today! Write out Hebrews 11:6 and James 1:25.

❏ Are you sick of repeating the same sin over and over? This is the Year of the Breakthrough and you can join the other captives that have been set free, but you must stop laying down sin with sin, and start using God's power and His Spirit. Write out specific examples of how you have used sin to try to lay down sin and why it did not work.

Lesson 4

❑ If you continue to use your own power, in the end you will find yourself with just you and your food, you and your alcohol, you and your idol. You must be baptized with the Holy Spirit that leads you where God wants you to go. In what ways have you been blessed when you follow the Spirit? Keep this list close to remind you!

❑ In this day and age, we are so spoiled—we have cars to drive us at any time, TVs, computers, satellite radio, etc.—anything to tune out God at any time. What are your distractions that block you from slowing down and following the Holy Spirit?

❑ Jesus was sinless and He overcame by the Holy Spirit. He is our example for making this Breakthrough! Write out several examples of Jesus' life that challenge you to stay focused on following God's Spirit.

Prayer

We pray, O God, Father, to be totally emptied out. Father, please see that hands clapping mean that each and every person in here wants to be in the vine. Everyone wants to lay it down. And, O Father, O God, I pray for those hearts that are not going to humble themselves or lower their desires to move on. And I pray that all evil spirits, anyone caught up in a sin in the evil power from satan, that is there, that deceives, that power of lawlessness, that it goes far away, God—that they will be healed today. I pray that they will confess this and get it out. Get these demons, God, that are going against You far out of this place and from this people, God. And I pray that as we hang onto hands here and we hang onto hands through the class, O God, to all of those saints out there that are hanging on, that they will see that there is no choice but one choice and that is purity and nothing else will be tolerated here. Because Your Spirit will walk. You will walk among us and You will lead us, guide us, protect us and bless us. We love this power, God, and we care nothing of the world. May the world all burn. All we care about, O God, is this connection: Your Spirit. Your will. Not talking about it, but doing it. All of this—we pray to be totally faithful, totally pure. The power of the purity, O God, is what we pray for this group. May all those that don't know what they are doing be exposed. May we all take correction and do nothing but Your will from this day until Jesus comes back. Through Your powerful name, Jesus, and Your power, and through the power that You had and the power of Your resurrection, Amen.

Answered Prayers

You can breakthrough into this freedom of being connected to God's Spirit, hour by hour, by constant input and then constant praying and then looking for the answered prayers. Write in your journal your answered prayers from this week.

BREAKTHROUGH Series

Day: _____

Hour by Hour

Finding the Spirit of God

Hour	Wait for God's lead?	Comments
6:00 AM	☐ Yes ☐ No	
7:00 AM	☐ Yes ☐ No	
8:00 AM	☐ Yes ☐ No	
9:00 AM	☐ Yes ☐ No	
10:00 AM	☐ Yes ☐ No	
11:00 AM	☐ Yes ☐ No	
12:00 PM	☐ Yes ☐ No	
1:00 PM	☐ Yes ☐ No	
2:00 PM	☐ Yes ☐ No	
3:00 PM	☐ Yes ☐ No	
4:00 PM	☐ Yes ☐ No	
5:00 PM	☐ Yes ☐ No	
6:00 PM	☐ Yes ☐ No	
7:00 PM	☐ Yes ☐ No	
8:00 PM	☐ Yes ☐ No	
9:00 PM	☐ Yes ☐ No	
10:00 PM	☐ Yes ☐ No	
11:00 PM	☐ Yes ☐ No	
Middle of the night	☐ Yes ☐ No	

Could you have done a better job today? Explain.

BreakthroughSeries.org   WeighDown.com

BREAKTHROUGH Series

Day: _____

Hour by Hour

Finding the Spirit of God

Hour	Wait for God's lead?	Comments
6:00 AM	☐ Yes ☐ No	
7:00 AM	☐ Yes ☐ No	
8:00 AM	☐ Yes ☐ No	
9:00 AM	☐ Yes ☐ No	
10:00 AM	☐ Yes ☐ No	
11:00 AM	☐ Yes ☐ No	
12:00 PM	☐ Yes ☐ No	
1:00 PM	☐ Yes ☐ No	
2:00 PM	☐ Yes ☐ No	
3:00 PM	☐ Yes ☐ No	
4:00 PM	☐ Yes ☐ No	
5:00 PM	☐ Yes ☐ No	
6:00 PM	☐ Yes ☐ No	
7:00 PM	☐ Yes ☐ No	
8:00 PM	☐ Yes ☐ No	
9:00 PM	☐ Yes ☐ No	
10:00 PM	☐ Yes ☐ No	
11:00 PM	☐ Yes ☐ No	
Middle of the night	☐ Yes ☐ No	

Could you have done a better job today? Explain.

BreakthroughSeries.org   **WeighDown.com**

BREAKTHROUGH Series

Day: _____

Hour by Hour

Finding the Spirit of God

Hour	Wait for God's lead?	Comments
6:00 AM	☐ Yes ☐ No	
7:00 AM	☐ Yes ☐ No	
8:00 AM	☐ Yes ☐ No	
9:00 AM	☐ Yes ☐ No	
10:00 AM	☐ Yes ☐ No	
11:00 AM	☐ Yes ☐ No	
12:00 PM	☐ Yes ☐ No	
1:00 PM	☐ Yes ☐ No	
2:00 PM	☐ Yes ☐ No	
3:00 PM	☐ Yes ☐ No	
4:00 PM	☐ Yes ☐ No	
5:00 PM	☐ Yes ☐ No	
6:00 PM	☐ Yes ☐ No	
7:00 PM	☐ Yes ☐ No	
8:00 PM	☐ Yes ☐ No	
9:00 PM	☐ Yes ☐ No	
10:00 PM	☐ Yes ☐ No	
11:00 PM	☐ Yes ☐ No	
Middle of the night	☐ Yes ☐ No	

Could you have done a better job today? Explain.

BreakthroughSeries.org   WeighDown.com

BREAKTHROUGH Series

Day: _____

Hour by Hour

Finding the Spirit of God

Hour	Wait for God's lead?	Comments
6:00 AM	☐ Yes ☐ No	
7:00 AM	☐ Yes ☐ No	
8:00 AM	☐ Yes ☐ No	
9:00 AM	☐ Yes ☐ No	
10:00 AM	☐ Yes ☐ No	
11:00 AM	☐ Yes ☐ No	
12:00 PM	☐ Yes ☐ No	
1:00 PM	☐ Yes ☐ No	
2:00 PM	☐ Yes ☐ No	
3:00 PM	☐ Yes ☐ No	
4:00 PM	☐ Yes ☐ No	
5:00 PM	☐ Yes ☐ No	
6:00 PM	☐ Yes ☐ No	
7:00 PM	☐ Yes ☐ No	
8:00 PM	☐ Yes ☐ No	
9:00 PM	☐ Yes ☐ No	
10:00 PM	☐ Yes ☐ No	
11:00 PM	☐ Yes ☐ No	
Middle of the night	☐ Yes ☐ No	

Could you have done a better job today? Explain.

BreakthroughSeries.org   WeighDown.com

Day: _____

BREAKTHROUGH Series

HOUR BY HOUR

Finding the Spirit of God

Hour	Wait for God's lead?	Comments
6:00 AM	☐ Yes ☐ No	
7:00 AM	☐ Yes ☐ No	
8:00 AM	☐ Yes ☐ No	
9:00 AM	☐ Yes ☐ No	
10:00 AM	☐ Yes ☐ No	
11:00 AM	☐ Yes ☐ No	
12:00 PM	☐ Yes ☐ No	
1:00 PM	☐ Yes ☐ No	
2:00 PM	☐ Yes ☐ No	
3:00 PM	☐ Yes ☐ No	
4:00 PM	☐ Yes ☐ No	
5:00 PM	☐ Yes ☐ No	
6:00 PM	☐ Yes ☐ No	
7:00 PM	☐ Yes ☐ No	
8:00 PM	☐ Yes ☐ No	
9:00 PM	☐ Yes ☐ No	
10:00 PM	☐ Yes ☐ No	
11:00 PM	☐ Yes ☐ No	
Middle of the night	☐ Yes ☐ No	

Could you have done a better job today? Explain.

BREAKTHROUGHSERIES.ORG   WEIGHDOWN.COM

A Breakthrough Moment
Demanding What You Crave

If you have struggled, you must stop and search your heart to make sure that you are not willfully putting God to the test by demanding the food that you crave. "But they continued to sin against him, rebelling in the desert against the Most High. They willfully put God to the test by demanding the food they craved. They spoke against God, saying, 'Can God spread a table in the desert? When he struck the rock, water gushed out, and streams flowed abundantly. But can he also give us food? Can he supply meat for his people?' When the LORD heard them, he was very angry; his fire broke out against Jacob, and his wrath rose against Israel, for they did not believe in God or trust in his deliverance." [Psalm 78:17-22]

What is the matter? Do you not believe that God can really punish or be so angry that He allows what you fear? Have you never had dreams to warn you, that give you visions of devastation? Did you not know that where you see the word "devastation" in the Bible, you see the word "sudden" right alongside it? Once He has had it with those who put Him to the test and demand what they crave, you have seen them given over. Your full repentance can tarry no longer.

Do not test the generous boundaries that God has given. The volume of food you are allowed to eat is generous. Willingly cut back where needed. Over the centuries, man-made religions would have "zero tolerance" for alcohol. Be grateful that you get to have wine at all. Cut back where needed. Fast from it if it has mastered you. Check to see if you can fast from it—perhaps it has mastered you?

Do not crave anything but a relationship with God through Christ. This is putting God to the test; in other words, it is stipulating that God is to have mercy on you while you willingly rebel against what He wants. This is insisting on getting God to die to His will so that you can have yours! This is dictating to God that He let you have your appetite and then giving God an ultimatum that He not exercise his wrath. It is expecting forgiveness.

Forgiving someone for wrongs is emotional and draining and time consuming. How much forgiveness have you demanded from God? Stop...get this right today. You stop demanding from God and demand obedience for yourself. You can obey today if you want to. You had better stop asking God to die to His will and die to yours.

Do not crave anything but a relationship with God through Christ.

Weekly Checklist

- ❏ Read your "Confession & Commitment" page every day
- ❏ Watch Video Five in class
- ❏ Listen to Audio Five
- ❏ Add to your Breakthrough Convictions & Breakthrough Lifestyle Changes Charts
- ❏ Add to your Blessings for Obedience & Curses for Disobedience Charts
- ❏ Make notes in your *BREAKTHROUGH* Journal
- ❏ Answer Week Five Daily Thought Questions
- ❏ Use your Reinforcement Resources & Truth Cards
- ❏ Fill in your Hour By Hour Chart
- ❏ Journal your Answered Prayers
- ❏ As you feel led, fill out the Weight Chart

Reinforcement Resources

- ❏ *The Tablet* — Read chapter 17 entitled "Suffering"
- ❏ *Rise Above* — Read Chapter 7 entitled "Backstroking the Red Sea"
- ❏ *Constant Encouragement* — Listen to "Saved From Self" Year 2, Volume 14
- ❏ *Laying Down Your Idols Devotional* — Read July 10th "Be on your Watch"
- ❏ *Constant Encouragement* — Listen to "Last Hour" Year 1, Volume 49
- ❏ *Hosanna Symphony* Soundtrack — Listen to "Another Time"

Scriptures

- ❏ Romans 13:1-2
- ❏ John 19:8-11
- ❏ John 12:23-28
- ❏ James 1:13-15
- ❏ John 12:20-26
- ❏ John 12:31-36

Lesson Five

For This Hour

*H*ave you surrendered every bite of food to the lead of the Heavenly Father? Why not? The answer is anti-authority. Co-existence, equal authority, is the song of liberty of satan. Since America loves her liberty and believes that authority is heresy or anti-religious, most Americans never find this essential concept. This week's lesson is to help you with the understanding and practice of following the lifestyle of Jesus Christ, who stayed under authority during suffering. Your Savior, Jesus Christ, did not choose His rule, but He chose God's rule in and up to His final hour.

This practice will be ground-breaking! As you have let go of control, you have begun to rejuvenate this fundamental relationship with God. God is our life. That statement means more to me with each passing day. I love God more and more and depend on His directions more with each passing day. I have only one regret in life and that is that I wish that I could have had a deeper relationship with God at an earlier age. I wish that someone had told me how not to depend on myself anymore.

John chapter 12 has a deep lesson for us all. Jesus replied, "The hour has come for the Son of Man to be glorified. I tell you the truth, unless a kernel of wheat falls to the ground and dies, it remains only a single seed. But if it dies, it produces many seeds. The man who loves his life will lose it, while the man who hates his life in this world will keep it for eternal life. Whoever serves me must follow me; and where I am, my servant also will be. My Father will honor the one who serves me. Now my heart is troubled, and what shall I say? 'Father, save me from this hour'? No, it was for this very reason I came to this hour. Father, glorify your name!"

Faith believes that there is a heavy directing hand from the Heavens on those in authority. Faith demands that you understand that a lack of peace is usually your own fault when it comes to authority —even if the person in authority is not perfect. If you wait for perfection in an authority as a reason to submit, you will never practice submission. Jesus told Pilate that He had no power over His life other than what was given by the Heavens. He submitted to the sentence of death on a cross, knowing His life was in the hands of God. In the presence of authority, even if it is your husband, you must keep your words few and Spirit-led and keep your expressions respectful and your focus and trust in the Creator. After you have perfected loving, faithful submission where the triangle is used daily, give it some time. Just wait and see. The wait is worth it. Everything will turn around. The uncommitted become committed.

So how do you commit to spouse or any authority? How do you commit to God? You lay down fears that you will be abused. Being under authority does not mean that women only find identity and meaning in their lives through their husbands and children. Just because Christ served the world under the authority of God, it does not mean that Christ lost His identity. So do not fear; satan is so against authority, calling the one in authority "teacher's pet" or making the person feel mindless. But getting under authority is genius, and what is more—it saves you. Being under authority has an ironic way of being quite the opposite. The person who loses himself in the will of his authority, has a way of being lifted up at work and brought into the spotlight and having nothing to fear. You have feared the wrong thing; you should fear your own rule or decisions for your eating and your life.

At some point, you are going to have to come to your hour, and your hour boils down to a decision of who is going to be glorified.

Who are you glorifying? Who are you supporting? Are you here to support yourself, or are you here to support Jesus Christ and God? And that is what all of life's questions boil down to. What is your motive for coming to church, for singing in the choir, for working on the decorating committee, for landscaping, for being on the tech team, for working as a leader or shepherd, or for counseling or teaching a class? What is your motive? Whose name are you glorifying and how do you know? Accepting marriage and the name of your husband and being submissive to the husband glorifies the husband's name and God's name. Whose name do you glorify in front of the children—yours or your husband's, satan's or God's? Whose name do you glorify at work—yours or your boss's?

So, why would someone struggle with their weight for years—even if they had been in Weigh Down Workshop and know of its concept of hunger and fullness for two to ten years? Why can you not just lose the weight?

Your excuses divert the real issue: Who is the God in your life? Who is the God in your eating? A lead is a lead. The God in the little things will be God in the big things. If you don't have a God in what you consider the little things, you don't have a God at all. It is not about big or small things, it is about *rule or no rule*.

You have come for this hour, to glorify His name, to glorify God's name, to glorify Christ's name. If you are eating when you're not hungry or eating beyond full, then you are glorifying your own name. That is futile, unproductive, useless, vain and empty; and glorifying yourself is repulsive—but worse, it is futile for you to have glorified something [yourself] that will be dead in a few years, and a being that has no power outside of being connected to God.

But how do you reverse this deep-seated sin? It is not easy. You must find your final hour—in other words YOUR hour of choice… THE HOUR that you will either glorify God or glorify yourself. This is your hour of commitment to NEVER go back and pick up your own eating habits, your own will, and your own desires. In your own final hour, you will be making the choice to get under God's rule or stay under your own self-rule. Which is it?

The test will be that you will want to have your excuse…but you must understand that EVERYONE has their test. Everyone has his or her problem. Stop the lie that your problem is bigger. God sets it up so it is a test for you to let Him rule and to let Him have control. Who is the God of the little things? This will let you know who will be your God of the big things.

Learn to say and practice, "NO, I will not rule my eating; I will not have my way; I will not diet; I will not control." You struggle because you have not told yourself "NO." You must choose God to lead you—say "NO" to leading yourself. Make this YOUR hour that you will say to God in your heart, "No more" to glorifying your own name!

If you are above authority, in reality you're down...

If you are under authority, in reality you're up.

Keep it to an hour by hour focus of glorifying God by saying "yes" to God and His lead. This is not hour-to-hour under your authority—this is hour to hour under God!

My prayer is that as you are reading this, you understand that the way to do this is making this choice of who rules your hour. You were born for this very hour of glorifying God over yourself. Everyone needs their own conclusive, irrevocable final hour. Amen—so be it!

Daily Thought Questions

❏ What has been the biggest revelation that hit your heart this week from the video? This is called a...
   BREAKTHROUGH CONVICTION.
Write these out and collect them over the next eight weeks. Record them each week and rewrite them on the permanent Breakthrough Conviction Chart in the front of the book. You can have several of these convictions per week. Make sure to go over these every week. Even if it seems stupid [that is satan's whisper], write them down. *Example: I am finally realizing that the only way to lose weight is to wait for true hunger each time.*

❏ Now take this *Breakthrough Conviction* and make a change in your life. When you make a small or big change in your lifestyle from these convictions it is called a...
   BREAKTHROUGH LIFESTYLE CHANGE.
Record them each week and rewrite them on the permanent Breakthrough Lifestyle Change Chart in the front of the book. Praise God for them and make sure you note the weight lifted off of you because you are changing to obey God rather than Self.

❏ REPETITION OF SINS MUST STOP. You may not get another chance to get it right. What sin are you repeating, and what have you done today to stop that?

BREAKTHROUGH

BLESSINGS FOR OBEDIENCE
- Praise God for the Breakthrough!!! Use this space to praise God for what He has done so far. Record these each week and rewrite them on the Blessings for Obedience Chart in the front of the book. How neat that the whole world is wonderful and life is worth living if we just focus on God for the day! *Example: I feel a heavy burden being lifted off my mind and body when I obey God.*

CURSES FOR DISOBEDIENCE
- Use this space for the unfortunate times that you take your eyes off of God. [Also rewrite them on the Curses for Disobedience Chart in the front of the book.] I have been at this for years, and I have seen that people are quick to forget the problems and curses that are caused by taking their eyes off of God. Make this a frequented page. It will turn you around before you binge.

- Did you deny head hunger this week? Did you eat with mouth hunger? Totally analyze your head hunger—with who, what, when, where, how, and why did it happen, and write this down.

LESSON 5

❏ Are you committed to an authority outside of yourself? [*Example: boss, husband, parent*]

❏ Describe your level of commitment and obedience and devotion to your authorities.

❏ Do you fall for the lie that it is okay not to obey authority if they are not a Christian or are not doing what you think that they should be doing?

❏ Do you believe that Romans 13 applies to Americans today? "Everyone must submit himself to the governing authorities, for there is no authority except that which God has established. The authorities that exist have been established by God. Consequently, he who rebels against the authority is rebelling against what God has instituted, and those who do so will bring judgment on themselves. For rulers hold no terror for those who do right, but for those who do wrong. Do you want to be free from fear of the one in authority? Then do what is right and he will commend you. For he is God's servant to do you good."

❏ According to the video lesson, what are the two things that need to be laid down in order to happily obey your authorities?

BREAKTHROUGH

- ❏ According to the video, what does this mean? "the man who loves his life will lose it, while the man who hates his life in this world will keep it for eternal life" [John 12:25]

- ❏ According to the video, what does this mean for us? "'Father save me from this hour?' No. It was for this very reason I came to this hour." [John 12:27]

- ❏ Galatians 5:16-18 says, "So I say, live by the Spirit, and you will not gratify the desires of the sinful nature. For the sinful nature desires what is contrary to the Spirit, and the Spirit what is contrary to the sinful nature. They are in conflict with each other, so that you do not do what you want. But if you are led by the Spirit, you are not under law."
  What is a deviant desire?

- ❏ Read Colossians 2:20: "Since you died with Christ to the basic principles of this world, why, as though you still belonged to it, do you submit to its rules: 'Do not handle! Do not taste! Do not touch!'? These are all destined to perish with use, because they are based on human commands and teachings. Such regulations indeed have an appearance of wisdom, with their self-imposed worship, their false humility and their harsh treatment of the body, but they lack any value in restraining sensual indulgence."

LESSON 5

❏ Are you more committed to man-made rules than God's rules? Think back to the man-made rules—the man-made diets. What were the harsh side effects? What did the years of devotion to man-made rules do for you?

❏ List how you have been destroyed by your false god(s).

❏ List the benefits you have experienced by being under God's rules.

- ❏ Write out examples of how your will has been or is different from God's will through any authority He has set up over you.

- ❏ Now contrast and write out areas where you have changed or are changing your will to match the authority's.

- ❏ Look back to your Commitment page. How are you doing on your commitment? What is the next time-consuming thing you have to give up so that you can get it right with God?

- ❏ Write down YOUR test—what is it that is your "final hour" of testing where God must be glorified? What is your excuse? What is the lie you are believing?

Lesson 5

- ❏ Is God in control of all the details of your day?

- ❏ How often do you REALLY pray about these details? This is a skill that will help you with going to God for everything. List out some parts of your day that you want to start praying about more.

- ❏ List your "do-gooder" tendencies that have kept you "busy" but not committed to God ruling and leading you.

- ❏ Who is the god in your life? Who is the god in your eating?

Prayer

O Father, God, we praise You for Jesus' words and for Your Spirit of interpretation. God, we praise You for the opportunity to understand this concept so that we can lose this empty life and find real life, so that we can not just be a single seed, God, but that we can produce many seeds. Father, we pray this to drive out the evil spirits and the spirits that are not under Your will. Father, may they all go away and out of this place and out of the hearts of Your people.

Father, may everyone understand that the way to do this is by making the choice, the choice of who rules their hour. I pray in the name of Jesus Christ that everyone here decides that they were born for the very hour of glorifying You over themselves. Father, help us all. Help us all to see how that choice completely puts a peace on the hour. It puts a peace on the day filled with these hours, and even one hour outside of Your will can eradicate, O God, and set us back from doing it Your way. Help us to see the joy in doing it Your way, oh God, so that we can glorify Your name and not our own anymore. And all this we beg and we pray in the name of Jesus Christ, Amen.

Answered Prayers

You can break through into this freedom of being connected to God's Spirit, hour by hour, by constant input, then constant praying, and then looking for the answered prayers. Write in your journal your answered prayers from this week.

Day: _____

BREAKTHROUGH

HOUR BY HOUR

Finding the Spirit of God

Hour	Wait for God's lead?	Comments
6:00 AM	☐ Yes ☐ No	
7:00 AM	☐ Yes ☐ No	
8:00 AM	☐ Yes ☐ No	
9:00 AM	☐ Yes ☐ No	
10:00 AM	☐ Yes ☐ No	
11:00 AM	☐ Yes ☐ No	
12:00 PM	☐ Yes ☐ No	
1:00 PM	☐ Yes ☐ No	
2:00 PM	☐ Yes ☐ No	
3:00 PM	☐ Yes ☐ No	
4:00 PM	☐ Yes ☐ No	
5:00 PM	☐ Yes ☐ No	
6:00 PM	☐ Yes ☐ No	
7:00 PM	☐ Yes ☐ No	
8:00 PM	☐ Yes ☐ No	
9:00 PM	☐ Yes ☐ No	
10:00 PM	☐ Yes ☐ No	
11:00 PM	☐ Yes ☐ No	
Middle of the night	☐ Yes ☐ No	

Could you have done a better job today? Explain.

BREAKTHROUGHSERIES.ORG   WEIGHDOWN.COM

BREAKTHROUGH

Day: _____

Hour by Hour
Finding the Spirit of God

Hour	Wait for God's lead?	Comments
6:00 AM	☐ Yes ☐ No	
7:00 AM	☐ Yes ☐ No	
8:00 AM	☐ Yes ☐ No	
9:00 AM	☐ Yes ☐ No	
10:00 AM	☐ Yes ☐ No	
11:00 AM	☐ Yes ☐ No	
12:00 PM	☐ Yes ☐ No	
1:00 PM	☐ Yes ☐ No	
2:00 PM	☐ Yes ☐ No	
3:00 PM	☐ Yes ☐ No	
4:00 PM	☐ Yes ☐ No	
5:00 PM	☐ Yes ☐ No	
6:00 PM	☐ Yes ☐ No	
7:00 PM	☐ Yes ☐ No	
8:00 PM	☐ Yes ☐ No	
9:00 PM	☐ Yes ☐ No	
10:00 PM	☐ Yes ☐ No	
11:00 PM	☐ Yes ☐ No	
Middle of the night	☐ Yes ☐ No	

Could you have done a better job today? Explain.

BreakthroughSeries.org   WeighDown.com

BREAKTHROUGH Series

Day: _____

Hour by Hour

Finding the Spirit of God

Hour	Wait for God's lead?	Comments
6:00 AM	☐ Yes ☐ No	
7:00 AM	☐ Yes ☐ No	
8:00 AM	☐ Yes ☐ No	
9:00 AM	☐ Yes ☐ No	
10:00 AM	☐ Yes ☐ No	
11:00 AM	☐ Yes ☐ No	
12:00 PM	☐ Yes ☐ No	
1:00 PM	☐ Yes ☐ No	
2:00 PM	☐ Yes ☐ No	
3:00 PM	☐ Yes ☐ No	
4:00 PM	☐ Yes ☐ No	
5:00 PM	☐ Yes ☐ No	
6:00 PM	☐ Yes ☐ No	
7:00 PM	☐ Yes ☐ No	
8:00 PM	☐ Yes ☐ No	
9:00 PM	☐ Yes ☐ No	
10:00 PM	☐ Yes ☐ No	
11:00 PM	☐ Yes ☐ No	
Middle of the night	☐ Yes ☐ No	

Could you have done a better job today? Explain.

BreakthroughSeries.org   WeighDown.com

BREAKTHROUGH Series

Day: _____

Hour by Hour
Finding the Spirit of God

Hour	Wait for God's lead?	Comments
6:00 AM	☐ Yes ☐ No	
7:00 AM	☐ Yes ☐ No	
8:00 AM	☐ Yes ☐ No	
9:00 AM	☐ Yes ☐ No	
10:00 AM	☐ Yes ☐ No	
11:00 AM	☐ Yes ☐ No	
12:00 PM	☐ Yes ☐ No	
1:00 PM	☐ Yes ☐ No	
2:00 PM	☐ Yes ☐ No	
3:00 PM	☐ Yes ☐ No	
4:00 PM	☐ Yes ☐ No	
5:00 PM	☐ Yes ☐ No	
6:00 PM	☐ Yes ☐ No	
7:00 PM	☐ Yes ☐ No	
8:00 PM	☐ Yes ☐ No	
9:00 PM	☐ Yes ☐ No	
10:00 PM	☐ Yes ☐ No	
11:00 PM	☐ Yes ☐ No	
Middle of the night	☐ Yes ☐ No	

Could you have done a better job today? Explain.

BreakthroughSeries.org WeighDown.com

BREAKTHROUGH Series

Day: _____

Hour by Hour
Finding the Spirit of God

Hour	Wait for God's lead?	Comments
6:00 AM	☐ Yes ☐ No	
7:00 AM	☐ Yes ☐ No	
8:00 AM	☐ Yes ☐ No	
9:00 AM	☐ Yes ☐ No	
10:00 AM	☐ Yes ☐ No	
11:00 AM	☐ Yes ☐ No	
12:00 PM	☐ Yes ☐ No	
1:00 PM	☐ Yes ☐ No	
2:00 PM	☐ Yes ☐ No	
3:00 PM	☐ Yes ☐ No	
4:00 PM	☐ Yes ☐ No	
5:00 PM	☐ Yes ☐ No	
6:00 PM	☐ Yes ☐ No	
7:00 PM	☐ Yes ☐ No	
8:00 PM	☐ Yes ☐ No	
9:00 PM	☐ Yes ☐ No	
10:00 PM	☐ Yes ☐ No	
11:00 PM	☐ Yes ☐ No	
Middle of the night	☐ Yes ☐ No	

Could you have done a better job today? Explain.

BreakthroughSeries.org   WeighDown.com

BREAKTHROUGH

A Breakthrough Moment
Tests vs. Trouble

Dear Lambs of God,

There is testing sometimes every day. God disciplines those whom He loves. Sometimes testing can feel shameful. Shame is by far one of the most awful feelings. God has promised to eventually remove shame and disgrace from His people, but doses of this are needed for humility.

The problem is that many a tender person can feel so downcast from discipline that they become depressed about it. This depression is from a feeling that God has forsaken you or given up on you. Thoughts might pass through your mind that He is passing you by and that you have lost your position with Him.

When my granddaughter Gracie was younger, if she stumbled, she always laughed and got right back up. But as she has gotten older, she has become overly embarrassed about it, and we have had to encourage her not to take it so hard, and we've had more trouble getting her right back on her feet. [Most of this has to do with missing a nap.] Nevertheless, one gets more aware of people when they get older and worry about what they think. A little one is just focused on the face of the parent. Adam and Eve had no shame before they sinned. Once they took their eyes off the Father and His will only—by looking sideways—they were aware of the eyes of others, and they hid out. Embarrassment is a feeling that drives one into covering up. In fact, the word "shame" actually means "to cover." Sometimes it takes this dreadful feeling for God to get through to us. Do not quit. You are loved—not forsaken. It has to be love—who else but God and Christ would bother to nudge you right back onto the right path? No one but God, and sometimes through correction from His Saints.

So, how do you get out of this?
- You must run to the Word of God and into His presence. Hasten to prayer and seek God's comfort. Get your mind off others.

- Repent from the mistake. MAKE PLANS THAT WILL HELP YOU TO AVOID THE SAME MISTAKE. This takes time and effort, so spend your time troubleshooting. For instance, if your problem is bingeing at home at night, make plans to go visit a Saint. Flee the place of temptation. Test your own actions.
- I know that humans are far more gentle inside than they appear on the outside. Many put on a tough exterior to hide the tenderness inside. Do not be afraid to open up to the trustworthy, dearest saints of God.
- Get back up. We are no different than children sometimes...we are resistant to receiving the comfort right away. We sometimes wallow [bathe, roll around, sit] in our pain. It is just a waste of time.
- Be merciful and help another Brother or Sister who is going through testing each and every time you get a chance. Galatians 6:1-3 says, "Brothers, if someone is caught in a sin, you who are spiritual should restore him gently. But watch yourself, or you also may be tempted. Carry each other's burdens, and in this way you will fulfill the law of Christ. If anyone thinks he is something when he is nothing, he deceives himself. Each one should test his own actions. Then he can take pride in himself, without comparing himself to somebody else, for each one should carry his own load."
- Expect testing and a lot of it. God is in a hurry to raise His children to maturity. Fasting from your sin, or just plain fasting, is a way to keep you alert and really ready if you seem caught up in a sin. Expect it today. Pass your test today. The shame will go away.

For the lambs of the gentle shepherd—Christ,

Weekly Checklist

- ❏ Read your "Confession & Commitment" page every day
- ❏ Watch Video Six in class
- ❏ Listen to Audio Six
- ❏ Add to your Breakthrough Convictions & Breakthrough Lifestyle Changes Charts
- ❏ Add to your Blessings for Obedience & Curses for Disobedience Charts
- ❏ Make notes in your *BREAKTHROUGH* Journal
- ❏ Answer Week Six Daily Thought Questions
- ❏ Use your Reinforcement Resources & Truth Cards
- ❏ Fill in your Hour By Hour Chart
- ❏ Journal your Answered Prayers
- ❏ As you feel led, fill out the Weight Chart

Reinforcement Resources

- ❏ *Rise Above*—Read Chapter 8 entitled "Hunger in the Desert"
- ❏ *Constant Encouragement*—Listen to "Staying in Step with the Spirit" Year 2, Volume 30
- ❏ *Ancient Paths*—Listen to Audio Lesson "Total Purity"
- ❏ *Exodus Out Of Egypt: The Change Series*—Listen to Audio Lesson 2 entitled "Focus"
- ❏ *Hosanna Symphony* Soundtrack—Listen to "Healing Well Wall"

Scriptures

- ❏ Ephesians 5:28-29
- ❏ I Corinthians 3:16-17
- ❏ Philippians 3:17-21
- ❏ I Corinthians 12
- ❏ I Peter 2:1-3
- ❏ Genesis 3:1-7
- ❏ Titus 2:11-13

Lesson Six

Don't Focus on the Body

Taking care of the body that God has so graciously given you is absolutely essential as a Christian. The body and soul and mind that you have been given is God's, and it belongs to God. In fact, another way to look at it is you are renting this body out. You have this time period with this body. He gives it to you, and you present this back to Him in the best condition that you can at Judgment Day.

Your eating is primarily an exercise for fuel. You will know that you are improving your intake by the amount of energy you feel.

You want to make sure you are not overmedicating the body; you want to make sure you are not overdrinking or taking anything that makes your body feel weird or feel sick from it. Anything that makes the body feel healthier, that's the direction you want to go. You're going to always see that eating smaller increments when the body calls for it is going to give you the optimum amount of energy. But if you neglect what God has given you, then God will destroy you because this focus on the body was never to bring men to it or the worry of men.

There are many people who are focused on the wrong body —many people are focused on their own bodies. If you will notice, focusing on your body is connected with sin. If you go to Genesis 3:1-7, it says:

Now the serpent was more crafty than any of the wild animals the LORD God had made. He said to the woman, "Did God really say, 'You must not eat from any tree in the garden'?" The woman said to the serpent, 'We may eat fruit from the trees in the garden,' but God did say, 'You must not eat fruit from the tree that is in the middle of the garden, and you must not touch it, or you will die.' 'You will not surely die,' the serpent said to the woman. 'For God knows that when you eat of it your eyes will be opened, and you will be like God, knowing good and evil.' When the woman saw that the fruit of the tree was good for food and pleasing to the eye, and also desirable for gaining wisdom, she took some and ate it. She also gave some to her husband, who was with her, and he ate it. Then the eyes of both of them were opened, and they realized they were naked; so they sewed fig leaves together and made coverings for themselves.

If you fall in love with yourself, then you will always be out of control. If you fall in love with God, then you will find the control.

Sin, touching the tree, is disobedience; and it is exactly what causes this focus on the body. So it's not a good thing. You may think, "I hate myself" or "I hate my body." But Paul tells us in Ephesians 5:28-29, "In this same way, husbands ought to love their wives as their own bodies. He who loves his wife loves himself. After all, no one ever hated his own body, but he feeds and cares for it, just as Christ does the church..."

People focusing on their own body in the wrong way become slanderous, hypocritical, full of malice, hate and envy. How do you rid yourself of that? By obeying the truth, by focusing off of that body and remembering that when you are focused on a body, the human body, you will be out of control. Paul wrote, "Join with others in following my example, brothers, and take note of those who live according to the pattern we gave you. For, as I have often told you before and now say again even with tears, many live as enemies of the cross of Christ. Their destiny is destruction, their god is their stomach, and their glory is in their shame. Their mind is on earthly things." [Philippians 3: 17-19] If you focus on Heaven, you will be in control and under that authority. If you fall in love with yourself, then you will always be out of control. If you fall in love with God, then you will find the control.

Stopping When You Are Full

How do you stop when there's a huge amount of food there? How do you stop when you are in the middle of a meal and you find yourself eating and eating and eating? How do you stop a binge? It's an entire life change. You stop the binge by an entire life change, because when you stop the focus on the physical body, you then focus on the body that we were called to focus on, which was the body of Christ. There's a body you can focus on that you don't gain weight from—indeed, it would be the opposite.

The Five "know/no's" so that you will not binge again:

1. **"Know thyself."** You will know yourself by your fruit, and don't lie to yourself anymore. When you know who you are, then you will be much more prepared.
2. **No diet foods.** Do not try to eat large volumes of empty calories. No extra chewing. No trying to make something else behave. No

going around telling everybody else what they need to do. No pointing fingers. Let go of blaming the food, and know that all the control is inside of you and that control comes from the right focus.

3. **No plans.** No control. Let go of control and allow your stomach to get empty. You don't know when that's going to be when you're losing weight. It isn't as routine as someone who's all the way down. You don't know when that "full" is going to be, so have no plans. Let go of control and just look for the Spirit of God and doing what He wants, and go back to being like a child.
4. **No binges.** If you're driving toward a binge, you're going down a familiar path of sitting down in front of the TV or whatever. It may be late at night or getting up at night when everybody has gone to bed and you go back. No! Grace teaches us to say "no."
5. **No self.** All of these things are saying "No" to self-focus on the body and "no" to focus on everyone else's body. So no envy, malice, slander, hate, projection, or tearing someone else down. That's between them and their God. You stay focused on your relationship between yourself and God and God's body of Christ.

Your weigh-ins can't be about you looking at what you need to lose or looking at your legs or looking at whatever. You may need to know a scale number for the fruit of what you're doing, but you don't need it for anything else, other than which direction you're going.

You have got to master this. You're not in this class to just halfheartedly do it. This is not just one more class. This truly is the Last Exodus. This is the last calling where God is calling you to master it; otherwise it's going to master you. Do not let a root grow up. You master self-denial and focusing on your own desires. No more focus on the wrong body. We are going to change our lives, and we are going to focus on the right body with the right self-control. We're going to get this. We're not going to give up, and we're going to get it right.

Daily Thought Questions

- What has been the biggest revelation that hit your heart this week from the video? This is called a...
  BREAKTHROUGH CONVICTION.
  Write these out and collect them over the next eight weeks. Record them each week and rewrite them on the permanent Breakthrough Conviction Chart in the front of the book. You can have several of these convictions per week. Make sure to go over these every week. Even if it seems stupid [that is satan's whisper], write them down. *Example: I am finally realizing that the only way to lose weight is to wait for true hunger each time.*

- Now take this *Breakthrough Conviction* and make a change in your life. When you make a small or big change in your lifestyle from these convictions it is called a...
  BREAKTHROUGH LIFESTYLE CHANGE.
  Record them each week and rewrite them on the permanent Breakthrough Lifestyle Change Chart in the front of the book. Praise God for them and make sure you note the weight lifted off of you because you are changing to obey God rather than Self.

- REPETITION OF SINS MUST STOP. You may not get another chance to get it right. What sin are you repeating, and what have you done today to stop that?

BLESSINGS FOR OBEDIENCE

- ❏ Praise God for the Breakthrough!!! Use this space to praise God for what He has done so far. Record these each week and rewrite them on the Blessings for Obedience Chart in the front of the book. How neat that the whole world is wonderful and life is worth living if we just focus on God for the day! *Example: I feel a heavy burden being lifted off my mind and body when I obey God.*

CURSES FOR DISOBEDIENCE

- ❏ Use this space for the unfortunate times that you take your eyes off of God. [Also rewrite them on the Curses for Disobedience Chart in the front of the book.] I have been at this for years, and I have seen that people are quick to forget the problems and curses that are caused by taking their eyes off of God. Make this a frequented page. It will turn you around before you binge.

- ❏ Did you deny head hunger this week? Did you eat with mouth hunger? Totally analyze your head hunger—with who, what, when, where, how and why did it happen, and write this down.

LESSON 6

❑ How important is your focus? What happens when you focus on yourself? What happens when you focus on Heaven?

❑ What "body" can you focus on that will help you lose weight and love God more? What does the Bible teach about correct focus on the physical body?

❑ Read Genesis 3. What happened when the woman and her husband ate from the tree? What caused the wrong focus on the human body?

❑ How do you feel when other people destroy your material possessions? Has anyone ever wrecked your car or damaged your property or borrowed your clothes and not returned them in good condition—or worse yet, never returned them? Compare this to how God must feel about what you have done to your body, mind and spirit in the past.

BREAKTHROUGH

- ❏ Read Ephesians 5:28-29. Many people say that they hate their body. Wouldn't you agree that what they really mean is that they hate the consequences of sin? When you lose the weight, you forget yourself, but when you sin you focus on the scales and your looks and your body. Time is wasted in looking for something to wear. We are to take care of our bodies. List the things you need to do to take care of the body God gave you. [Make sure that you do not start feeling sorry for self, but rather stay convicted that you have not taken good care of what you have been given.]

- ❏ How can you honor God and present your body in the best condition to Him?

- ❏ Read Philippians 3. Have you made your stomach a god? How are you going to change this?

- ❏ How do you rid yourself of slander, hypocrisy, malice, hate and envy?

Lesson 6

❏ What are the 5 "know/no's" and what are some immediate changes you are going to make to implement these?
1.

2.

3.

4.

5.

Changes:

❏ What does God's grace teach us, and how are you going to reflect that in your daily life?

❏ When you get on the scales, what is your purpose and what are you looking for?

❑ God is going to transform our lowly bodies in the end. Look at all the testimonies of people who lost their weight on the "20,000 pounds down" video. Everyone was transformed into something beautiful! Make sure you are focusing off the human body shape and focusing on obeying God. God will take care of your body if you take care of His Church body. Name some things that you can do for others over the next few weeks, and make this a daily focus!

❑ What are the things you are still vocalizing a complaint about? The traffic, your work reports, your kids, your time, your food? Now read I Corinthians 10:10, "And do not grumble, as some of them did—and were killed by the destroying angel." First Timothy 6:8 says, "But if we have food and clothing, we will be content with that."

Lay down your grumbling for this hour!

❑ List some ways you can slow down. How are some ways you can start over? Think about how to use the technology of cell phones, iPods, computer calendar reminders that "pop up" with alarms each hour to remind you to refocus.

LESSON 6

PRAYER

God, thank You for Your Spirit, for Your wisdom and for Your energy. It is the world that is giving up, and they are just down, and they do not know which way to go, Father. They are searching so hard for how to stay motivated. O God, You are motivating this class, and You are motivating it with Your Spirit, Your wisdom, and Your power; and Father when we turn to You, we are renewed, and when we wait on You we rise up with wings like eagles. God, help this group and these Saints who are bowing down to You, who want to be transformed, to be born anew. They want this new life. They do not want any longer to let their greed be their God. They don't want a life destined to destruction. They don't want to destroy Your temple, Father. They want to take care of it, Father. They don't want to focus on their own body, God. Help them to focus on Your Kingdom, Your body, the body of Christ.

Father, help us all to realize how beautiful it is that You have given us something to focus on, that You have given us salvation, that You have given us a way out of this old, empty life and given us a new life. Father, may this *BREAKTHROUGH* Class lose the commitment to their own desires and regain the commitment more every day to You, Your Kingdom, Your will and Your Spirit of self-control, taking care of Your body, Your Saints and Your people. In the meantime, God, I pray that You will continue to bless them in a powerful way for this change of mind, change of heart, change of life, change of soul and change of strength, that they have given it all over to You; and in the end they are blessed beyond blessed. May the world see it, God, so that You can be glorified so that all the people seeking You out can find their way home to Your Kingdom. In Jesus' name we pray for even more of Your Spirit, more wisdom and more energy as we employ it for the good of You. In Jesus' name we pray all this. Amen.

ANSWERED PRAYERS

Write in your journal your answered prayers from this week.

BREAKTHROUGH *Series*

Day: _____

Hour by Hour
Finding the Spirit of God

Hour	Wait for God's lead?	Comments
6:00 AM	☐ Yes ☐ No	
7:00 AM	☐ Yes ☐ No	
8:00 AM	☐ Yes ☐ No	
9:00 AM	☐ Yes ☐ No	
10:00 AM	☐ Yes ☐ No	
11:00 AM	☐ Yes ☐ No	
12:00 PM	☐ Yes ☐ No	
1:00 PM	☐ Yes ☐ No	
2:00 PM	☐ Yes ☐ No	
3:00 PM	☐ Yes ☐ No	
4:00 PM	☐ Yes ☐ No	
5:00 PM	☐ Yes ☐ No	
6:00 PM	☐ Yes ☐ No	
7:00 PM	☐ Yes ☐ No	
8:00 PM	☐ Yes ☐ No	
9:00 PM	☐ Yes ☐ No	
10:00 PM	☐ Yes ☐ No	
11:00 PM	☐ Yes ☐ No	
Middle of the night	☐ Yes ☐ No	

Could you have done a better job today? Explain.

BreakthroughSeries.org WeighDown.com

BREAKTHROUGH Series

Day: _____

Hour by Hour
Finding the Spirit of God

Hour	Wait for God's lead?	Comments
6:00 AM	☐ Yes ☐ No	
7:00 AM	☐ Yes ☐ No	
8:00 AM	☐ Yes ☐ No	
9:00 AM	☐ Yes ☐ No	
10:00 AM	☐ Yes ☐ No	
11:00 AM	☐ Yes ☐ No	
12:00 PM	☐ Yes ☐ No	
1:00 PM	☐ Yes ☐ No	
2:00 PM	☐ Yes ☐ No	
3:00 PM	☐ Yes ☐ No	
4:00 PM	☐ Yes ☐ No	
5:00 PM	☐ Yes ☐ No	
6:00 PM	☐ Yes ☐ No	
7:00 PM	☐ Yes ☐ No	
8:00 PM	☐ Yes ☐ No	
9:00 PM	☐ Yes ☐ No	
10:00 PM	☐ Yes ☐ No	
11:00 PM	☐ Yes ☐ No	
Middle of the night	☐ Yes ☐ No	

Could you have done a better job today? Explain.

BreakthroughSeries.org   WeighDown.com

BREAKTHROUGH Series

Day: _____

Hour by Hour
Finding the Spirit of God

Hour	Wait for God's lead?	Comments
6:00 AM	☐ Yes ☐ No	
7:00 AM	☐ Yes ☐ No	
8:00 AM	☐ Yes ☐ No	
9:00 AM	☐ Yes ☐ No	
10:00 AM	☐ Yes ☐ No	
11:00 AM	☐ Yes ☐ No	
12:00 PM	☐ Yes ☐ No	
1:00 PM	☐ Yes ☐ No	
2:00 PM	☐ Yes ☐ No	
3:00 PM	☐ Yes ☐ No	
4:00 PM	☐ Yes ☐ No	
5:00 PM	☐ Yes ☐ No	
6:00 PM	☐ Yes ☐ No	
7:00 PM	☐ Yes ☐ No	
8:00 PM	☐ Yes ☐ No	
9:00 PM	☐ Yes ☐ No	
10:00 PM	☐ Yes ☐ No	
11:00 PM	☐ Yes ☐ No	
Middle of the night	☐ Yes ☐ No	

Could you have done a better job today? Explain.

BreakthroughSeries.org   WeighDown.com

BREAKTHROUGH Series

Day: _____

HOUR BY HOUR
Finding the Spirit of God

Hour	Wait for God's lead?	Comments
6:00 AM	☐ Yes ☐ No	
7:00 AM	☐ Yes ☐ No	
8:00 AM	☐ Yes ☐ No	
9:00 AM	☐ Yes ☐ No	
10:00 AM	☐ Yes ☐ No	
11:00 AM	☐ Yes ☐ No	
12:00 PM	☐ Yes ☐ No	
1:00 PM	☐ Yes ☐ No	
2:00 PM	☐ Yes ☐ No	
3:00 PM	☐ Yes ☐ No	
4:00 PM	☐ Yes ☐ No	
5:00 PM	☐ Yes ☐ No	
6:00 PM	☐ Yes ☐ No	
7:00 PM	☐ Yes ☐ No	
8:00 PM	☐ Yes ☐ No	
9:00 PM	☐ Yes ☐ No	
10:00 PM	☐ Yes ☐ No	
11:00 PM	☐ Yes ☐ No	
Middle of the night	☐ Yes ☐ No	

Could you have done a better job today? Explain.

BREAKTHROUGHSERIES.ORG WEIGHDOWN.COM

BREAKTHROUGH *Series*

Day: _____

Hour by Hour
Finding the Spirit of God

Hour	Wait for God's lead?	Comments
6:00 AM	☐ Yes ☐ No	
7:00 AM	☐ Yes ☐ No	
8:00 AM	☐ Yes ☐ No	
9:00 AM	☐ Yes ☐ No	
10:00 AM	☐ Yes ☐ No	
11:00 AM	☐ Yes ☐ No	
12:00 PM	☐ Yes ☐ No	
1:00 PM	☐ Yes ☐ No	
2:00 PM	☐ Yes ☐ No	
3:00 PM	☐ Yes ☐ No	
4:00 PM	☐ Yes ☐ No	
5:00 PM	☐ Yes ☐ No	
6:00 PM	☐ Yes ☐ No	
7:00 PM	☐ Yes ☐ No	
8:00 PM	☐ Yes ☐ No	
9:00 PM	☐ Yes ☐ No	
10:00 PM	☐ Yes ☐ No	
11:00 PM	☐ Yes ☐ No	
Middle of the night	☐ Yes ☐ No	

Could you have done a better job today? Explain.

BREAKTHROUGHSERIES.ORG　　　　　WEIGHDOWN.COM

A Breakthrough Moment
Mind Over Matter

Dearest Saints in the World,

How grateful I am to have another day to live out the principles of Christ Jesus. He was perfect every day in His walk with God. Our happiness today is one-half perspective and one-half action. When you get your mind right, you will conquer your actions. It is "mind over matter," not "matter over mind."

1] Prepare the mind with the right perspective: If you stop for 10 minutes and contemplate that you are mortal and you have more than you deserve in just waking up, it will change your outlook and therefore your day. Can you believe that you exist and that you have been given breath—along with a heartbeat—and on top of that, it is mixed with freedom to think and love and obey God! All of these blessings come with an opportunity to live forever with a moral, good God! You might have to stop several times per day to fill your mind with this perspective. Set up an automatic reminder on your phone, or email/calendar, or have a close friend call you regularly for a time. You must get into the habit of returning to this perspective.

The Muslims turn to God five times per day. I was in Egypt and saw this with my own eyes. I could hear the loud wailing to God across the land at noon each day. Everyone stopped what they were doing, whether they were eating, working, or walking down the road. We would have to stop filming, and everyone would face the east and pray out loud. My life has been so full of difficult spiritual warfare that it has trained me to pray many times per day and go to God for many things. The more you see that you cannot control anyone or anything in life, the more you will pray. This is a good thing. Each prayer builds faith. Without a doubt, each of you has a good heart. I know this, for each time you stop and think about the right, humble perspective, you melt and get right back on the path of good. The problem comes in the distractions. You must not let life or any

BREAKTHROUGH

man distract you from the need to stop in the day and get the right perspective. In your contemplation, prepare your mind for a test. Imagine yourself standing in the wind of the test and not bending. You deserve a test, and humility is the answer. Mind over matter.

2] Mind over matter will change the deeds of the day: if we get up and humble ourselves before God and man, we will not expect anyone to be nice to us or anyone to return our love. However, if you prepare the next 14 hours to be positive, good hours of loving others and helping others no matter what they do or say, you will eventually receive abundant love. If you look to God alone for praise and direction, you will not look for the praise of man or attention from man—but the irony is that you will get positive feedback. If you fall and look to man for approval, you will not receive it, and this will send you into depression or anger or frustration or laziness and vindictiveness. Nothing positive will come from looking to man or life to give you something back. It will not only be a negative day, it might even be a cursed day. But if you look only to the Heavens and talk only to true Saints about perspectives, you will find yourself getting encouragement from God and man. If you only want God's approval, you will not care about man's approval. A Saint's approval and man's approval are two entirely different things. God's pat on the back and answered prayers and an encouraging word from a Saint give you the energy to do right. In turn, you will soon have so many positive days that you can then encourage other Saints to do right. This builds a life worth living.

This mind over matter gives you reason to live. Depression comes from failure to maintain the right perspective. Failure comes from not preparing your mind. The answer: take the time to prepare the mind and heart, and you will love the day that God has given you! You will know that you have arrived when you have constant thankfulness.

Perspectives mixed with actions: we do not deserve another chance to obey. Pray for more fear to never repeat an offense to God. God's patience wears thin, and you see the need to give people over to their own devices. Pray that today is not that day, and live your day like this is the last day. Get it right, for you might meet Jesus tomorrow. Always prepare yourself to meet your Maker.

If you are stumbling, it is because you are not putting enough effort into preparing your mind for humility. Each person should know how much it takes to make it through lunch and then how much it takes to make it to bedtime to have a positive, grateful, thankful, obedient heart.

All eagles are renowned for their excellent eyesight. Its sharpness is at least four times that of a person with perfect vision. The eagle can identify a rabbit moving almost a mile away. We need to sharpen our spiritual eyesight so that we can detect the enemy.

Pray today and for this upcoming testing week for each Saint to stop and prepare their heart and mind for perfect actions. Don't you realize that the world does not know this secret, and they watch you to see how you stay positive? They are thankful only for a moment in the midst of self-gratification. Then they are miserable. We are thankful all day long—all week long! Thanksgiving does not come just one day out of the year; it is every day. It is a way of life. Pray that we can live this life and live long enough to show others the way out of the darkness.

A Servant of God,

Weekly Checklist

- ❑ Read your "Confession & Commitment" page every day
- ❑ Watch Video Seven in class
- ❑ Listen to Audio Seven
- ❑ Add to your Breakthrough Convictions & Breakthrough Lifestyle Changes Charts
- ❑ Add to your Blessings for Obedience & Curses for Disobedience Charts
- ❑ Make notes in your *BREAKTHROUGH* Journal
- ❑ Answer Week Seven Daily Thought Questions
- ❑ Use your Reinforcement Resources & Truth Cards
- ❑ Fill in your Hour By Hour Chart
- ❑ Journal your Answered Prayers
- ❑ As you feel led, fill out the Weight Chart

Reinforcement Resources

- ❑ *The Tablet*—Read chapter 21 entitled "The Narrow Door"
- ❑ *Rise Above*—Read Chapter 6 entitled "Secrets of the Prison"
- ❑ *Weigh Down Advanced*—Listen to Audio Lesson 4 entitled "Christian Perspective"
- ❑ *Ancient Paths*—Listen to Audio entitled "Self-Focus, Self-Pity, and Depression"
- ❑ *Hosanna Symphony* Soundtrack—Listen to "You'll Make It Through"
- ❑ *Laying Down Your Idols Devotional*—Read November 11th "You Cannot Camouflage Your Heart"

Scriptures

- ❑ John 14:28-31
- ❑ John 4:31-34
- ❑ James 1:5-8
- ❑ Romans 9:19-21
- ❑ Romans 7:21-24
- ❑ II Timothy 3:1-7

Lesson Seven

Purposeful Responsibility

*C*an you believe that you are alive in a free country and are able to bow down to God and worship him freely? Look at you—you are breathing this morning! Look around you—you have loving brothers and sisters in Christ at Weigh Down who are an email or phone call away. We have the unbelievable opportunity to choose a purposeful responsibility.

It is true that years of sin will have led to entanglements that seem overwhelming to unravel, but it is a lie that it cannot be accomplished and in an expedient way. When you have not accepted personal responsibility for all of your life and actions and directions, you run the risk of becoming the chronic projector, and you run the risk that you never open up or trust anyone. This can lead to paranoia and panic attacks. You project your own sins onto others and exaggerate them in order to justify your own sins. This judgmental spirit becomes a mindset, and you eventually run off the people nearest and dearest to you. This can all be reversed by a simple refocusing this very minute.

When you do not take responsibility, there is a strong probability of you masking your pain with harmful substances. If you keep this up, it eventually destroys your life and your family's lives. Not taking responsibility will affect everything: your relationship with God and therefore, your marriage, your outside relationships, your job, your health, your children. Others run the risk of blaming God and circumstances to the point that they ruin their life with anger and/or being overcome with depression. There are only curses left for those who avoid the choice of purposeful responsibility.

However, when you choose to make this brilliant choice on a daily basis, you become joyful and delightful and it makes you merciful toward others. You will actually be interested in others again, and you will feel favor from everyone around you. The Heavenly favor returns.

How hard is it for you? Will it be hard in the beginning? Yes, but only in the beginning. It gets much easier with every right choice you make. You will have no memory of your former desires anymore than a young child remembers wanting to run out into a busy street. Your desires will die out, and you will learn to take your pain to God—the God of any and all comfort. That is why you have not felt enough comfort—you have not gone to God enough. Try it today and see if God will not give you a clear mind, wisdom for direction, and an unexplained deep comfort from your anxiousness.

We can choose to take our pain to God, and then we are set to take responsibility for our actions, feelings, and our words that will start to gush with love. You will actually start to L-O-V-E life!

Are you overwhelmed by fears? You must first stop blaming others, blaming circumstances, blaming God, blaming inequity, and blaming past sins. You must stop depending on people or some "mystery missing inspiration or fact or phenomenon" to save you. You have what you need to walk out the first half of the day. Then stop during midday [before or after the lunch hour], and get your head back on straight again. Go over your purpose to live for God and Christ, and know that a huge, massive crowd in Heaven is cheering you on with a powerful God who will give you that power through prayer just because you made the right choice.

Again, be afraid of being double-minded, where one day you are "on" and the next day you are "off." This comes from a weak will that likes to give in to selfish desires. When you are weighed down by SELF DIRECTION you lose THE DIRECTION, and therefore, you will experience humiliation and embarrassment. The wrong choice is exhausting. You will have to fight hard in the beginning.

> *The most successful people in the world have one purpose. They narrow down their interests. They consolidate or merge all that they have — mind, heart, strength and soul for living into one goal — ONE goal. With this single, driving goal, they make their mark on earth.*

Jesus Christ got up each day and chose THE DIRECTION, and the result was that he was widely known by everyone before he died, even appearing in front of the highest government offices in the nation of Israel and the worldwide powers in Rome. Jesus Christ created a religious revolution and started a church that would turn the world upside down, and he did all of this inside a 3-year ministry with 12 men who were of little help, for they were not sure yet of his goals; and in fact one was so selfish that he wanted money and approval from the local government rather than the approval from Christ. [Of course, these men wound up following Christ and evangelizing the world.]

How did Jesus do it? He had that resolute focus on ONE purpose, and He depended on God alone and His enormous permanent empire.

Take responsibility for your life this hour with powerful help from the Heavens. Once you taste this purposeful responsibility, you will lay down the empty life you have been leading.

BREAKTHROUGH

Daily Thought Questions

- What has been the biggest revelation that hit your heart this week from the video? This is called a...
            BREAKTHROUGH CONVICTION.
Write these out and collect them over the next eight weeks. Record them each week and rewrite them on the permanent Breakthrough Conviction Chart in the front of the book. You can have several of these convictions per week. Make sure to go over these every week. Even if it seems stupid [that is satan's whisper], write them down. *Example: I am finally realizing that the only way to lose weight is to wait for true hunger each time.*

- Now take this *Breakthrough Conviction* and make a change in your life. When you make a small or big change in your lifestyle from these convictions it is called a...
            BREAKTHROUGH LIFESTYLE CHANGE.
Record them each week and rewrite them on the permanent Breakthrough Lifestyle Change Chart in the front of the book. Praise God for them and make sure you note the weight lifted off of you because you are changing to obey God rather than Self.

- REPETITION OF SINS MUST STOP. You may not get another chance to get it right. What sin are you repeating, and what have you done today to stop that?

LESSON 7

BLESSINGS FOR OBEDIENCE
- ❏ Praise God for the Breakthrough!!! Use this space to praise God for what He has done so far. Record these each week and rewrite them on the Blessings for Obedience Chart in the front of the book. How neat that the whole world is wonderful and life is worth living if we just focus on God for the day! *Example: I feel a heavy burden being lifted off my mind and body when I obey God.*

CURSES FOR DISOBEDIENCE
- ❏ Use this space for the unfortunate times that you take your eyes off of God. [Also rewrite them on the Curses for Disobedience Chart in the front of the book.] I have been at this for years, and I have seen that people are quick to forget the problems and curses that are caused by taking their eyes off of God. Make this a frequented page. It will turn you around before you binge.

- ❏ Did you deny head hunger this week? Did you eat with mouth hunger? Totally analyze your head hunger—with who, what, when, where, how, and why did it happen, and write this down.

BREAKTHROUGH

- ❑ How do you rate yourself in terms of taking personal responsibility for all actions and life choices? [10 is the highest and 0 is the lowest score] _____

- ❑ Make a list of things in life that you take responsibility for. *Example: I make sure that the bills are paid every month.*

- ❑ Make a list of things that you do not take enough responsibility for. *Example: I count on the Weigh Down Coordinator to help me lose weight.*

- ❑ According to this week's lecture, what is the mindset of people who have not accepted personal responsibility?

- ❑ Read the points on the following page and underline all the excuses that you have used on yourself to avoid taking personal responsibility for your actions:

LESSON 7

- **BLAME OTHERS:** It's not my fault that I am the way that I am. My parents raised me wrongly—they overfed me, they never taught me boundaries, and they pushed food on me. My parents made me who I am today. My husband is driving me to food. My job is stressing me out. My children are driving me to overdrink and overeat. My wife is responsible for my affair.

- **BLAME CIRCUMSTANCES:** If only I had better luck and had been born to a healthier family or attended a better school or gotten a better job, etc. If only I didn't stay home with the kids all day long. If only I had a different body structure. Life is so depressing. No matter how hard I work, I will never get ahead because I was dealt such a bad hand.

- **BLAME GOD:** How can you say I am responsible for what happens to me in the future? Fate, luck, providence, and huge forces beyond my control have a greater bearing on my future than I have. Romans 9:19: "...why does God still blame us?" I never asked to be born. God made me this way. Romans 7:24: "What a wretched man I am."

- **BLAME INEQUITY:** God has asked too much of me. There is no way I'll ever be able to handle all of this. Life is unfair! There is no sense in trying to take control of my life. Why go on; I see no use in life because the troubles and the problems will never cease.

- **BLAME PAST SINS:** How can I ever be forgiven, seeing how bad my life has been? Others are so far ahead of me spiritually...I will never be like them. I have been the worst sinner, and God does not want me anymore. I don't have a relationship with God like I used to. I cannot seem to get this relationship with God back—what is the use in trying anymore? I am unworthy.

BREAKTHROUGH

- ❑ All 5 projection categories lead to self-pity. How often/frequently do you claim that others/God/circumstances have determined what you are today?

- ❑ How frequently do you feel sorry for yourself or feel like a victim?

- ❑ How easy is it to return to a projectionist/victim mindset?

- ❑ What changes are you going to make to redirect this mindset?

- ❑ Who have you been depending upon for life choices? Who will you choose now to depend upon?

- ❑ What have you turned to for comfort—food, alcohol, spending, etc.? Use the space provided to write out the pain of these addictions and what they have done to ruin your life and your family's lives:

LESSON 7

❑ Have you experienced anger? If so, then you might be guilty of blaming God. [Why? Because if you would get angry or frustrated with your earthly authorities, then you would do the same thing to God. In fact, it is God that allows every experience in your life.] If you experience anger, make sure that you repent before God and start looking inward. List your anger episodes over the last few months.

❑ Look up II Corinthians 1:3-4. Who should you turn to for comfort when you are in need? Write the verse out and post it in the kitchen, pantry, or work station.

❑ Each time you feel the urge to fill up your life with food, alcohol, cigarettes, self-pity, spending, talking too much, indulgences, etc.—STOP. Instead, realize that "more" is NOT better. Count your blessings and fill up your life with a relationship with God. [The way to put this into practice is by seeking and obeying God's commands.]

171

BREAKTHROUGH

- ❏ Have you experienced panic attacks or paranoia? Do you have a problem trusting people? According to the lecture, what is the cause of this and how do you overcome this mindset?

- ❏ Accepting personal and purposeful responsibility [according to the lecture] includes what?

- ❏ Do you believe that it IS a choice that you can make to lose all your weight or to lay down any selfish lust or addictive substances? ❏ Yes ❏ No

- ❏ Mark the following lines that are applicable:
  By turning to God and making a choice to choose purposeful responsibility:
    - ❏ I will control my eating.
    - ❏ I will control my drinking.
    - ❏ I will stop the binge eating.
    - ❏ I will no longer feel sorry for myself.
    - ❏ I will control my thoughts and surrender my mind to higher and more noble thoughts, and I will stop blaming others.
    - ❏ I will stop overly depending on others.
    - ❏ I will turn to God for comfort when fearful, empty, lonely, depressed, ready to party, hurting, or lost.
    - ❏ I will take the necessary steps or make the necessary changes that I need to make to overcome.
    - ❏ I will put even more effort into returning to the basics [Week One] and starting over if I have messed up.
    - ❏ I will commit to this path of glorifying God over all other desires or selfish wants!

Lesson 7

Prayer

Father, we come before you and we bow our heads before You; and God, we pray for all the saints who are dedicating their lives, who are committing their lives, and who are breaking through, God. Please, Father, may this continue to be.

May this commitment grow so that everyone who has things to work on will be moved. Father, thank You for those working on the video footage who have lost weight, the camera people who have lost weight, God. We're hearing that everyone even touching one of the CDs, that you are anointing this, and we cannot do this without You. You are everything, and all anointing comes from You. And God, we just praise You for the blessings—all the things that have been going on—I can't believe it, God. The list is endless, all that You are doing to fight back the enemies and to bring forth Your Saints. What a day we're living in, and may we live up to it. May we get on this train, this work that You are doing, God, that is starting to move faster and faster ahead.

May everyone be, after this class, more dedicated than ever before, taking purposeful responsibility for their lives and following Christ all the way so that they can join the massive Heavenly Kingdom and movement that is going on in Heaven with You and all of the witnesses who have come before us. We praise You for this opportunity to join that and to be trained for that team. May we do it justice. In Jesus' name, Amen.

Answered Prayers

You can break through into this freedom of being connected to God's Spirit, hour by hour, by constant input, then constant praying, and then looking for the answered prayers. Write in your journal your answered prayers from this week.

BREAKTHROUGH Series

Day: _____

Hour by Hour
Finding the Spirit of God

Hour	Wait for God's lead?	Comments
6:00 AM	☐ Yes ☐ No	
7:00 AM	☐ Yes ☐ No	
8:00 AM	☐ Yes ☐ No	
9:00 AM	☐ Yes ☐ No	
10:00 AM	☐ Yes ☐ No	
11:00 AM	☐ Yes ☐ No	
12:00 PM	☐ Yes ☐ No	
1:00 PM	☐ Yes ☐ No	
2:00 PM	☐ Yes ☐ No	
3:00 PM	☐ Yes ☐ No	
4:00 PM	☐ Yes ☐ No	
5:00 PM	☐ Yes ☐ No	
6:00 PM	☐ Yes ☐ No	
7:00 PM	☐ Yes ☐ No	
8:00 PM	☐ Yes ☐ No	
9:00 PM	☐ Yes ☐ No	
10:00 PM	☐ Yes ☐ No	
11:00 PM	☐ Yes ☐ No	
Middle of the night	☐ Yes ☐ No	

Could you have done a better job today? Explain.

BreakthroughSeries.org   WeighDown.com

BREAKTHROUGH Series

Day: _____

Hour by Hour

Finding the Spirit of God

Hour	Wait for God's lead?	Comments
6:00 AM	☐ Yes ☐ No	
7:00 AM	☐ Yes ☐ No	
8:00 AM	☐ Yes ☐ No	
9:00 AM	☐ Yes ☐ No	
10:00 AM	☐ Yes ☐ No	
11:00 AM	☐ Yes ☐ No	
12:00 PM	☐ Yes ☐ No	
1:00 PM	☐ Yes ☐ No	
2:00 PM	☐ Yes ☐ No	
3:00 PM	☐ Yes ☐ No	
4:00 PM	☐ Yes ☐ No	
5:00 PM	☐ Yes ☐ No	
6:00 PM	☐ Yes ☐ No	
7:00 PM	☐ Yes ☐ No	
8:00 PM	☐ Yes ☐ No	
9:00 PM	☐ Yes ☐ No	
10:00 PM	☐ Yes ☐ No	
11:00 PM	☐ Yes ☐ No	
Middle of the night	☐ Yes ☐ No	

Could you have done a better job today? Explain.

BreakthroughSeries.org   WeighDown.com

BREAKTHROUGH *Series*

Day: _____

Hour by Hour
Finding the Spirit of God

Hour	Wait for God's lead?	Comments
6:00 AM	☐ Yes ☐ No	
7:00 AM	☐ Yes ☐ No	
8:00 AM	☐ Yes ☐ No	
9:00 AM	☐ Yes ☐ No	
10:00 AM	☐ Yes ☐ No	
11:00 AM	☐ Yes ☐ No	
12:00 PM	☐ Yes ☐ No	
1:00 PM	☐ Yes ☐ No	
2:00 PM	☐ Yes ☐ No	
3:00 PM	☐ Yes ☐ No	
4:00 PM	☐ Yes ☐ No	
5:00 PM	☐ Yes ☐ No	
6:00 PM	☐ Yes ☐ No	
7:00 PM	☐ Yes ☐ No	
8:00 PM	☐ Yes ☐ No	
9:00 PM	☐ Yes ☐ No	
10:00 PM	☐ Yes ☐ No	
11:00 PM	☐ Yes ☐ No	
Middle of the night	☐ Yes ☐ No	

Could you have done a better job today? Explain.

BREAKTHROUGHSERIES.ORG			WEIGHDOWN.COM

Day: _____

BREAKTHROUGH Series

Hour by Hour

Finding the Spirit of God

Hour	Wait for God's lead?	Comments
6:00 AM	☐ Yes ☐ No	
7:00 AM	☐ Yes ☐ No	
8:00 AM	☐ Yes ☐ No	
9:00 AM	☐ Yes ☐ No	
10:00 AM	☐ Yes ☐ No	
11:00 AM	☐ Yes ☐ No	
12:00 PM	☐ Yes ☐ No	
1:00 PM	☐ Yes ☐ No	
2:00 PM	☐ Yes ☐ No	
3:00 PM	☐ Yes ☐ No	
4:00 PM	☐ Yes ☐ No	
5:00 PM	☐ Yes ☐ No	
6:00 PM	☐ Yes ☐ No	
7:00 PM	☐ Yes ☐ No	
8:00 PM	☐ Yes ☐ No	
9:00 PM	☐ Yes ☐ No	
10:00 PM	☐ Yes ☐ No	
11:00 PM	☐ Yes ☐ No	
Middle of the night	☐ Yes ☐ No	

Could you have done a better job today? Explain.

BreakthroughSeries.org   WeighDown.com

BREAKTHROUGH Series

Day: _____

HOUR BY HOUR
Finding the Spirit of God

Hour	Wait for God's lead?	Comments
6:00 AM	☐ Yes ☐ No	
7:00 AM	☐ Yes ☐ No	
8:00 AM	☐ Yes ☐ No	
9:00 AM	☐ Yes ☐ No	
10:00 AM	☐ Yes ☐ No	
11:00 AM	☐ Yes ☐ No	
12:00 PM	☐ Yes ☐ No	
1:00 PM	☐ Yes ☐ No	
2:00 PM	☐ Yes ☐ No	
3:00 PM	☐ Yes ☐ No	
4:00 PM	☐ Yes ☐ No	
5:00 PM	☐ Yes ☐ No	
6:00 PM	☐ Yes ☐ No	
7:00 PM	☐ Yes ☐ No	
8:00 PM	☐ Yes ☐ No	
9:00 PM	☐ Yes ☐ No	
10:00 PM	☐ Yes ☐ No	
11:00 PM	☐ Yes ☐ No	
Middle of the night	☐ Yes ☐ No	

Could you have done a better job today? Explain.

BreakthroughSeries.org　　　　WeighDown.com

A Breakthrough Moment
One Resolute Purpose

Dearest Brothers and Sisters,

Praise God for another day to declare to the heavens and the earth, "God is everything!" Remember that one of the most defining characteristics of Jesus Christ is that He had ONE PURPOSE. The most successful people in the world have one purpose. They narrow down their interest, their drive, their reason for living into one goal. With this single driving goal, they make their mark on earth.

Jesus said it all on the cross, but He verbally expressed it in John 14: "You heard me say, 'I am going away and I am coming back to you.' If you loved me, you would be glad that I am going to the Father, for the Father is greater than I. I have told you now before it happens, so that when it does happen you will believe. I will not speak with you much longer, for the prince of this world is coming. He has no hold on me, but the world must learn that I love the Father and that I do exactly what my Father has commanded me.'"

The Prince of this world had NO HOLD on Christ. Christ's head was not turned by the world nor by the commands of satan. Not satan, but GOD held Jesus' heart. The world—the whole world—had to learn that Christ did EXACTLY what God commanded Him. He did not have divided interests, and so He was extremely successful in reaching His goal.

Then in John 4:31-34 it says, "Meanwhile his disciples urged him, "Rabbi, eat something." But he said to them, 'I have food to eat that you know nothing about.'" Then his disciples said to each other, "Could someone have brought him food?" "My food," said Jesus, "is to do the will of him who sent me and to finish his work."

Like Job, the word and will of God was better than his daily bread. His food, His sustenance, His enjoyment, and His life were renourished when He was helping others find God and find the truth [God's work].

He was focused so that He was not vacillating back and forth on what the purpose of the day was. When your goal is your own desires or satan's will, it leaves you empty—quick thrills followed with horrible guilt, pain, emptiness, curses and problems. In contrast, God's will leaves you with better health, better family life, more friends, and peace and joy and more desire to live. James warns of the double-minded men in James 1:5-8,

> "If any of you lacks wisdom, he should ask God, who gives generously to all without finding fault, and it will be given to him. But when he asks, he must believe and not doubt, because he who doubts is like a wave of the sea, blown and tossed by the wind. That man should not think he will receive anything from the Lord; he is a double-minded man, unstable in all he does."

Paul warns of the weak-willed women in II Timothy 3:6-7,

> "They are the kind who worm their way into homes and gain control over weak-willed women, who are loaded down with sins and are swayed by all kinds of evil desires, always learning but never able to acknowledge the truth."

Unstable people who turn their eyes and their heads toward the offerings of this world are WEAK-WILLED. They are loaded down with their own desires. These desires must change. I have seen people who want to change, turn their double-minded ways into ONE FOCUS, ONE PURPOSE and never go back. It starts as an hourly choice and then becomes a daily choice and then becomes a PERMANENT RESOLUTE PURPOSE. You have to abandon one and focus on another. Abandon any base, simplistic, pointless desires that waste your time and your energy and wear your heart and soul out. The wrong choice is exhausting.

Again, Jesus Christ was known by all before He died, even appearing in front of the highest in government offices in the nation of Israel and Rome. Jesus Christ created a religious revolution and started a church that would turn the world upside down, and all of this inside 33 years of life. What have you done with your life?

What has your double focus accomplished? Change today and be successful by choosing ONE PURPOSE. Paul followed suit, and all those that follow suit will be well known by the Heavens and all the witnesses that have gone before us. It is a greatly successful crowd that will now live forever.

A Servant of God,

Weekly Checklist

- ❑ Read your "Confession & Commitment" page every day
- ❑ Watch Video Eight in class
- ❑ Listen to Audio Eight
- ❑ Add to your Breakthrough Convictions & Breakthrough Lifestyle Changes Charts
- ❑ Add to your Blessings for Obedience & Curses for Disobedience Charts
- ❑ Make notes in your *BREAKTHROUGH* Journal
- ❑ Answer Week Eight Daily Thought Questions
- ❑ Use your Reinforcement Resources & Truth Cards
- ❑ Fill in your Hour By Hour Chart
- ❑ Journal your Answered Prayers
- ❑ As you feel led, fill out the Weight Chart

Reinforcement Resources

- ❑ *The Tablet*—Read chapter 23 entitled "All Or Nothing"
- ❑ *Exodus Out of Egypt: The Change Series*—Listen to original Audio 4 entitled "Stay Awake"
- ❑ *Laying Down Your Idols Devotional*—Read December 13th "Live By the Spirit"
- ❑ *Constant Encouragement*—Listen to "Staying in Step with the Spirit" Year 2, Volume 30
- ❑ *Legend to The Treasure* Soundtrack—Listen to "This Covenant"
- ❑ Re-read your own answered prayers and "Breakthrough" moments from your Breakthrough Journal

Scriptures

- ❑ Revelations 2:1-5
- ❑ Proverbs 28:25
- ❑ II Chronicles 6:14
- ❑ Romans 12:1-8
- ❑ James 5:13-16
- ❑ I Corinthians 13

Lesson Eight
Breakthrough Moments

    This series started as a class that would be committed to the "ALL" that Jesus knew needed to be a part of our life. 'Hear, O Israel, the Lord our God, the Lord is one. Love the Lord your God with all your heart and with all your soul and with all your mind and with all your strength." Mark 12:29-30 Without the ALL—you have nothing. The average seeker of God stops short of giving everything and leaves a "high place" or "stronghold" in their life. A stronghold is an area in your life that you want to control and manage. It looks like the child who does not want to give up his toy and throws a temper tantrum when asked to give up the toy. The toy is fun, and the toy is filling up the child's mind and interest. But after all, it is just a toy and the child is fine in a few minutes after sacrificing the toy.

    Even your high places or strongholds must be given over. This is not usually done voluntarily, but after suffering. If you could only just concentrate on the suffering that comes from holding on to that stronghold in your life; or in other words, not giving God ALL of your heart, soul, mind and strength. No one can give up your stronghold for you. No class, no person, no legion of demons can make you give it up. YOU have to take personal responsibility for giving up and giving ALL.

This is the type of class that never really spiritually stops once you begin. We have acknowledged God in this class. Heaven rules, so we have experimented with letting go of control. Are you still letting go, or was that only a temporary venture for the fun of it? One might think that letting go and letting God is just a good suggestion — but it is fundamental to opening the whole spiritual world and being able to fight the demons of the spiritual world.

Letting go of ALL CONTROL is connected to everything. Once you let go of all control, you can start over with a new life and be born again. You will no doubt be a whole new person with control and no anger or greed or pride. You may feel silly because you become more childlike and happier and giddy, but you have no more miserable, wretched, bad-mood days. We have found a relationship with God, and to find this relationship you have to lose not only controlling your life, but lose an intimate relationship with the world. We have found that it is the most priceless and precious thing in the world to surrender all to God Almighty. You will want to find others who are on this quest. So, what do you say? Are you sick of suffering and living a shameful life? Are you worried about the day that you meet your Maker at all? Are you concerned that you are wasting time, that time is running out and that you are living day in and day out with no purpose or real meaning? Are you sick to the death of being a fake? Conviction in the night has carried you this far. In the end, your conscience and body and mind will lead you, because the weight will be too heavy for you to bear. You will want to end the anger and loneliness. It is all wearing you out. Call upon God when you are worn out, and Breakthrough! A lot of weight will be lifted. This weight is too heavy for you. Give it up! Give it up! End your hopelessness by knowing that it is all an hour by hour choice. Hebrews 8:7-13 says:

> "For if there had been nothing wrong with that first covenant, no place would have been sought for another. But God found fault with the people and said: 'The time is coming, declares the Lord, when I will make a new covenant with the house of Israel and with the house of Judah. It will not be like the covenant I made with their forefathers when I took them by the hand to lead them

out of Egypt, because they did not remain faithful to my covenant, and I turned away from them, declares the Lord. This is the covenant I will make with the house of Israel after that time, declares the Lord. I will put my laws in their minds and write them on their hearts. I will be their God, and they will be my people. No longer will a man teach his neighbor, or a man his brother, saying, "Know the Lord," because they will all know me, from the least of them to the greatest. For I will forgive their wickedness and will remember their sins no more.' By calling this covenant 'new,' he has made the first one obsolete; and what is obsolete and aging will soon disappear."

The whole purpose of the new covenant is the ALL. We cannot repeat history. We must remain totally faithful to the end. The suffering will lead us to let go, and the letting go of control will change us. ...

"Consider that our present sufferings are not worth comparing with the glory that will be revealed in us. The creation waits in eager expectation for the sons of God to be revealed. For the creation was subjected to frustration, not by its own choice, but by the will of the one who subjected it, in hope that the creation itself will be liberated from its bondage to decay and brought into the glorious freedom of the children of God." We know that the whole creation has been groaning as in the pains of childbirth right up to the present time. Not only so, but we ourselves, who have the first fruits of the Spirit, groan inwardly as we wait eagerly for our adoption as sons, the redemption of our bodies." Romans 8:18

Does the test all boil down to power? The irony is that when you try to take over to get power, you lose the power. If you give up the control, you gain power and friends and help and love

We can change together as we fill up on God instead of the food. When you change from one glory to another, you become closer to one another and happier every day than you were the day before! We know the path, and we know how to stay on it. When there is suffering, we now know where to go—to the God of all comfort. I love God more and more every day. There is an answer; there is a way out! We have found it, and we are never going back.

We have found a way to fill up on God rather than the world, and because of it, we have been in a constant state of change — changing from one glory to another glory.

Daily Thought Questions

❏ What has been the biggest revelation that hit your heart this week from the video? This is called a...
 BREAKTHROUGH CONVICTION.
Write these out and collect them over the next eight weeks. Record them each week and rewrite them on the permanent Breakthrough Conviction Chart in the front of the book. You can have several of these convictions per week. Make sure to go over these every week. Even if it seems stupid [that is satan's whispers], write them down. *Example: I am finally realizing that the only way to lose weight is to wait for true hunger each time.*

❏ Now take this *Breakthrough Conviction* and make a change in your life. When you make a small or big change in your lifestyle from these convictions it is called a...
 BREAKTHROUGH LIFESTYLE CHANGE.
Record them each week and rewrite them on the permanent Breakthrough Lifestyle Change Chart in the front of the book. Praise God for them and make sure you note the weight lifted off of you because you are changing to obey God rather than Self.

❏ REPETITION OF SINS MUST STOP. You may not get another chance to get it right. What sin are you repeating, and what have you done today to stop that?

BLESSINGS FOR OBEDIENCE

☐ Praise God for the Breakthrough!!! Use this space to praise God for what He has done so far. Record these each week and rewrite them on the Blessings for Obedience Chart in the front of the book. How neat that the whole world is wonderful and life is worth living if we just focus on God for the day! *Example: I feel a heavy burden being lifted off my mind and body when I obey God.*

CURSES FOR DISOBEDIENCE

☐ Use this space for the unfortunate times that you take your eyes off of God. [Also rewrite them on the Curses for Disobedience Chart in the front of the book.] I have been at this for years, and I have seen that people are quick to forget the problems and curses that are caused by taking their eyes off of God. Make this a frequented page. It will turn you around before you binge.

☐ Did you deny head hunger this week? Did you eat with mouth hunger? Totally analyze your head hunger—with who, what, when, where, how, and why did it happen, and write this down.

LESSON 8

❏ How have you done so far? Before this class, how long had your weight hit a "plateau" or how long had it been since there was any weight loss [if applicable to you]?

❏ Take the entire 8 weeks and choose your most remarkable "Breakthrough" moment! Write it here:

❏ This week's lesson features several exciting testimonies of those who have COMMITTED to God and to this class, among which you can now count yourself! Write one or two things that "stuck out"—convicted or encouraged you the most—about these people's lives.

Testimony One:

Testimony Two:

Testimony Three:

Testimony Four:

Testimony Five:

❏ Read Proverbs 14:25 and 24:26. We have learned not to run from or avoid godly friends and authorities, but to seek them out! God will bless these relationships. Who are people that you know will point you straight up to God? Give them a call this week or take them to lunch! Surrounding yourself with the Truth and with godly company is crucial to keeping your focus completely on our Wonderful Creator!

❑ Remember and make a list of worldly things that have called your name since starting this class.

Now, step back and realize how completely futile and empty all these pursuits are! If it helps you, keep the above list with you and add everything each temptation ultimately robs you of.

❑ Letting go of control is a major theme in this class. In what areas have you laid this down and let God Almighty have control in your life? [Marriage, job, etc.] In what [if any] areas do you still need to let Him rule?

❑ Write down the wonderful blessings, especially spiritually, that come when you give God control! How do you feel better?

Lesson 8

- [ ] Jesus Christ is our ultimate example who gave up control in ALL areas of his life, and now He is sitting at the right hand of God. Ponder and dwell on His attitude and selflessness, and the results!

- [ ] Why is pride such a scary thing? What does it lead to?

- [ ] We have the "Mystery" of Christ that allows true Peace, Joy and Love! What is this mystery? [Colossians 2:2-3]

- [ ] We have an extremely merciful God, even when we have been stubborn. Read Deuteronomy 21 and pray that He will reveal any stubbornness you may still have!

- [ ] We have all grieved God's Spirit and grieved Christ. But God has given [you] a second chance!! This is All or Nothing. Look up the definition of "all" and write it down below.

BREAKTHROUGH

- Take the Breakthrough Conviction page and the Breakthrough Lifestyle page and write out what lifestyle changes you continued to make up through the eighth week. Next, write out the lifestyle changes that you have dropped and need to pick back up. Go back and read your Commitment statement to God and rededicate your heart, soul, mind, and strength to this new life!

Prayer

Father, we want You, not the food. We want this relationship, not the food relationship. We want Your approval, not the world's approval. Father, we want You. You are the morning, and You are the noon and You are the night. You are the beginning and the end. You are the Alpha and the Omega. You are everything, God. We pray in the name of Jesus Christ that everyone in here transfers successfully a relationship with themselves and the food over to a relationship with You and Your Kingdom. May everything else, [of course it will be], be added unto them as they made this transfer. I pray it will be clear to them. I pray this will be something they want and that they will realize, in analyzing their wants, what's really at the core of their lives and that they repent and make You their first love.

All this we pray through Christ who showed us about first loves—Jesus Christ who went all the way to the death showing us that His love for You was greater than His love for Himself or for things in the world or for food or for glory—for anything. He would take the lowliest and the last seat, the worst death, the worst reputation, the "nothing" jobs. He would take everything that was considered nothing on earth, from His birthplace to His death. He would take nothing, but He would make one thing His "something," and that was You, God. From doing that and making that choice, He turned out to be the most exalted name on earth—Jesus Christ—and the most known person and the most popular. God, may we all join in and make this earth and what's on this earth nothing, but make You our something. And all this we pray, we pray this O God, because this is very serious, a very serious choice. I pray that everyone sees clearly to make You their everything. And all this we pray in Jesus' name, Amen.

Answered Prayers

Write in your journal your answered prayers from this week.

BREAKTHROUGH Series

Day: _____

Hour by Hour
Finding the Spirit of God

Hour	Wait for God's lead?	Comments
6:00 AM	☐ Yes ☐ No	
7:00 AM	☐ Yes ☐ No	
8:00 AM	☐ Yes ☐ No	
9:00 AM	☐ Yes ☐ No	
10:00 AM	☐ Yes ☐ No	
11:00 AM	☐ Yes ☐ No	
12:00 PM	☐ Yes ☐ No	
1:00 PM	☐ Yes ☐ No	
2:00 PM	☐ Yes ☐ No	
3:00 PM	☐ Yes ☐ No	
4:00 PM	☐ Yes ☐ No	
5:00 PM	☐ Yes ☐ No	
6:00 PM	☐ Yes ☐ No	
7:00 PM	☐ Yes ☐ No	
8:00 PM	☐ Yes ☐ No	
9:00 PM	☐ Yes ☐ No	
10:00 PM	☐ Yes ☐ No	
11:00 PM	☐ Yes ☐ No	
Middle of the night	☐ Yes ☐ No	

Could you have done a better job today? Explain.

BreakthroughSeries.org   WeighDown.com

BREAKTHROUGH Series

Day: _____

Hour by Hour
Finding the Spirit of God

Hour	Wait for God's lead?	Comments
6:00 AM	☐ Yes ☐ No	
7:00 AM	☐ Yes ☐ No	
8:00 AM	☐ Yes ☐ No	
9:00 AM	☐ Yes ☐ No	
10:00 AM	☐ Yes ☐ No	
11:00 AM	☐ Yes ☐ No	
12:00 PM	☐ Yes ☐ No	
1:00 PM	☐ Yes ☐ No	
2:00 PM	☐ Yes ☐ No	
3:00 PM	☐ Yes ☐ No	
4:00 PM	☐ Yes ☐ No	
5:00 PM	☐ Yes ☐ No	
6:00 PM	☐ Yes ☐ No	
7:00 PM	☐ Yes ☐ No	
8:00 PM	☐ Yes ☐ No	
9:00 PM	☐ Yes ☐ No	
10:00 PM	☐ Yes ☐ No	
11:00 PM	☐ Yes ☐ No	
Middle of the night	☐ Yes ☐ No	

Could you have done a better job today? Explain.

BreakthroughSeries.org WeighDown.com

BREAKTHROUGH Series

Day: _____

Hour by Hour
Finding the Spirit of God

Hour	Wait for God's lead?	Comments
6:00 AM	☐ Yes ☐ No	
7:00 AM	☐ Yes ☐ No	
8:00 AM	☐ Yes ☐ No	
9:00 AM	☐ Yes ☐ No	
10:00 AM	☐ Yes ☐ No	
11:00 AM	☐ Yes ☐ No	
12:00 PM	☐ Yes ☐ No	
1:00 PM	☐ Yes ☐ No	
2:00 PM	☐ Yes ☐ No	
3:00 PM	☐ Yes ☐ No	
4:00 PM	☐ Yes ☐ No	
5:00 PM	☐ Yes ☐ No	
6:00 PM	☐ Yes ☐ No	
7:00 PM	☐ Yes ☐ No	
8:00 PM	☐ Yes ☐ No	
9:00 PM	☐ Yes ☐ No	
10:00 PM	☐ Yes ☐ No	
11:00 PM	☐ Yes ☐ No	
Middle of the night	☐ Yes ☐ No	

Could you have done a better job today? Explain.

BreakthroughSeries.org   WeighDown.com

BREAKTHROUGH Series

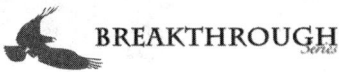

Day: _____

HOUR BY HOUR
Finding the Spirit of God

Hour	Wait for God's lead?	Comments
6:00 AM	☐ Yes ☐ No	
7:00 AM	☐ Yes ☐ No	
8:00 AM	☐ Yes ☐ No	
9:00 AM	☐ Yes ☐ No	
10:00 AM	☐ Yes ☐ No	
11:00 AM	☐ Yes ☐ No	
12:00 PM	☐ Yes ☐ No	
1:00 PM	☐ Yes ☐ No	
2:00 PM	☐ Yes ☐ No	
3:00 PM	☐ Yes ☐ No	
4:00 PM	☐ Yes ☐ No	
5:00 PM	☐ Yes ☐ No	
6:00 PM	☐ Yes ☐ No	
7:00 PM	☐ Yes ☐ No	
8:00 PM	☐ Yes ☐ No	
9:00 PM	☐ Yes ☐ No	
10:00 PM	☐ Yes ☐ No	
11:00 PM	☐ Yes ☐ No	
Middle of the night	☐ Yes ☐ No	

Could you have done a better job today? Explain.

BREAKTHROUGHSERIES.ORG WEIGHDOWN.COM

BREAKTHROUGH

Day: _____

Hour by Hour
Finding the Spirit of God

Hour	Wait for God's lead?	Comments
6:00 AM	☐ Yes ☐ No	
7:00 AM	☐ Yes ☐ No	
8:00 AM	☐ Yes ☐ No	
9:00 AM	☐ Yes ☐ No	
10:00 AM	☐ Yes ☐ No	
11:00 AM	☐ Yes ☐ No	
12:00 PM	☐ Yes ☐ No	
1:00 PM	☐ Yes ☐ No	
2:00 PM	☐ Yes ☐ No	
3:00 PM	☐ Yes ☐ No	
4:00 PM	☐ Yes ☐ No	
5:00 PM	☐ Yes ☐ No	
6:00 PM	☐ Yes ☐ No	
7:00 PM	☐ Yes ☐ No	
8:00 PM	☐ Yes ☐ No	
9:00 PM	☐ Yes ☐ No	
10:00 PM	☐ Yes ☐ No	
11:00 PM	☐ Yes ☐ No	
Middle of the night	☐ Yes ☐ No	

Could you have done a better job today? Explain.

BreakthroughSeries.org   WeighDown.com

LESSON 8

A Breakthrough Moment
Preening for Purity

Dear Saints,

How do you purify your life and your heart and mind so that it is always clean? This is something that takes constant work. Just as you shower every day, you must take the time to wash out your mind and heart. All animals preen and wash themselves. An eagle spends up to one third of his day preening his feathers. These animals are early to bed and early to rise, and this does keep them in the will of the Father and out of trouble. Read how Hezekiah, a young man of 25, purified a nation of people and God's Temple…

"Hezekiah was twenty-five years old when he became king, and he reigned in Jerusalem twenty-nine years. His mother's name was Abijah daughter of Zechariah. He did what was right in the eyes of the LORD, just as his father David had done. In the first month of the first year of his reign, he opened the doors of the temple of the LORD and repaired them. He brought in the priests and the Levites, assembled them in the square on the east side and said: "Listen to me, Levites! Consecrate yourselves now and consecrate the temple of the LORD, the God of your fathers. Remove all defilement from the sanctuary. Our fathers were unfaithful; they did evil in the eyes of the LORD our God and forsook him. They turned their faces away from the LORD's dwelling place and turned their backs on him. They also shut the doors of the portico and put out the lamps. They did not burn incense or present any burnt offerings at the sanctuary to the God of Israel. Therefore, the anger of the LORD has fallen on Judah and Jerusalem; he has made them an object of dread and horror and scorn, as you can see with your own eyes. This is why our fathers have fallen by the sword and why our sons and daughters and our wives are in captivity. Now I intend to make a covenant with the LORD, the God of Israel, so that his fierce anger will turn away from us. My sons, do not be negligent now, for the LORD has chosen you to stand before him and serve him, to minister before him and to burn incense..." When they had assembled their brothers and consecrated themselves, they went in to purify the temple of the LORD, as the king had ordered, following the word of the LORD. The priests went into the sanctuary of the LORD to purify it. They brought out to the courtyard of the LORD's temple everything unclean that they found in the temple of the LORD. The Levites took it and carried it out to the Kidron Valley. They began the consecration on the first day of the first month, and by the eighth day of the month they reached the portico of the LORD. For eight more days they consecrated the temple of the LORD itself, finishing on the sixteenth day of the first month. Then they went in to King Hezekiah and reported: "We have purified the entire temple of the LORD, the altar of burnt offering with all its utensils, and the table for setting out the consecrated bread, with all its articles. We have prepared and consecrated all the articles that King Ahaz removed in his unfaithfulness while he was king. They are now in front of the LORD's altar. Early the next morning King Hezekiah gathered the city officials together and went up to the temple of the LORD. They brought seven bulls, seven rams, seven male lambs and seven male goats as a sin offering for the kingdom, for the sanctuary and for Judah. The king commanded the priests, the descendants of Aaron, to offer these on the altar of the LORD...He stationed the Levites in the temple of the LORD with cymbals, harps and lyres in the way prescribed by David and Gad the king's seer and Nathan the prophet; this was commanded by the LORD through his prophets. So the Levites stood ready with David's instruments, and the priests with their trumpets. Hezekiah gave the order to sacrifice the burnt offering on the altar. As the offering began, singing to the LORD began also, accompanied by trumpets and the instruments of David king of Israel. The whole assembly bowed in worship, while the singers sang and the trumpeters played. All this continued until the sacrifice of the burnt offering was completed. When the offerings were finished, the king and everyone present with him knelt down and worshiped. King Hezekiah and his officials ordered the Levites to praise the LORD with the words of David and of Asaph the seer. So they sang praises with gladness and bowed their heads and worshiped. Then Hezekiah said, "You have now dedicated yourselves to the LORD. Come and bring sacrifices and thank offerings to the temple of the LORD." So the assembly brought sacrifices and thank offerings, and all whose hearts were willing brought burnt offerings. There were burnt offerings in abundance, together with the fat of the fellowship offerings and the drink offerings that accompanied the burnt offerings. So the service of the temple of the LORD was reestablished. Hezekiah and all the people rejoiced at what God had brought about for his people, because it was done so quickly." II Chronicles 29

How convicting to see a community work together to get the entire Temple prepared and cleaned up and to see everyone come before the Lord with humbled hearts readied 1) to be prayed over with the blood of lambs [this took time to perform before God], 2) to sing and worship and bow down, 3) to bow in worship while the singers sang and trumpeters played 4) after performing the sacrifices to God, for the leaders to kneel down and worship and then sing and then bow their heads in more worship. The service to God was reestablished with rejoicing! What a picture of worship. How could we go wrong with services of pure worship? This group of people took a bath. Go through every room in your heart, and remove the darkness and trash it in the Kidron Valley. Get it far away. Do not go places that are associated with sin. Flee from evil and get AWAY from it—remove it from your life once and for all. Life is too short and sin is too deadly. Join with Hezekiah, a young man who said "No" to evil and unclean and "Yes!" to living a clean, pure, white life of worshiping God alone. What if, like the eagle, it took up to 1/3 of your waking hours to be totally pure before God? So what? That is what it takes to assure that the eagle soars above the earth. Replace plotting evil with preening for purity.

Your servant and sister,

BREAKTHROUGH

All directed by The God of the Universe through willing vessels.
Author/Director/Producer: Gwen Shamblin

A special thanks to Assistant Directors Amy Stites and Joe Langsdon and the video and audio editing team: Michelle McDonald, Erin Moore, David Martin, B.B. Barcus, Erin Shamblin, Elizabeth Hannah, and Ryan McCauley.

A special thanks to Michael Shamblin and True Religion Records for the song "Pure Sunday," used in this series; underscoring by Michael Shamblin, B.B. Barcus, and Tish Dunn. The *BREAKTHROUGH* Series class also inspired Matt Weaver to write the song "Committed to the Cause," and Julie Radebaugh to write "I Want You," which were both used in these lessons.

Of course, we couldn't have done this without the MIS team, including Eldon Gormsen, and Marc Dunn, and the Outreach and Administrative team, including Tedd Anger, Candace Anger, Regina Smith, Jessica Walters, Jenni Mendl, Jennifer Martin, Abigail McDonald, and Laura Gormsen.

We also want to thank the Weigh Down Auxiliary Production Staff: Brandon Hannah, Elisabeth Miller, Jonathan Walters, Anique Leaman, Beth Ancona, Greg MacPherson, Robert Zanoni, Pam Gunger, Phyllis Eikenberry, Ruth Beld, Andrew Langsdon, Calvin Voorhis, Erik Gadke, Jason Abelt, Josh Vick, Jonathan Hagans, Justin Rockwell, Kris Kubichar, Kyle Davis, Luke Higgins, Nathan Abelt, Rich Friesen, Robbie Ruble, Ryan Sisemore, Scott Sabo, Sheldon Singh, Todd Kubiak, Tracey Herron, Wesley Henry, Derek Davis, Jake Gormsen, Mike Wheeler, Nic Hord, Austin Polivka, Carmen D'Amato, Carol Whitney, Jill Snapp, Lisa Roth, Bonnie Hennessy, Cassandra Beiling, Chloe Leaman, Judy Tuxford, Mary Beld, Melanie Titus, Michael Hagans, Monica Weaver, Pam Friesen, Rachel Zanoni, Sally Neely, Tracy Carson, Terri Harless, Vickie Tennyson.

A special thanks to the Weigh Down staff and the Auxiliary staff!

Breakthrough Moments

photography by Anique Leaman and Abigail McDonald

Adoration

Freedom to Worship

Committed to God

New Life

Born Again

Breakthrough

God is Everything

Strong Leaders

Worship

Innocence

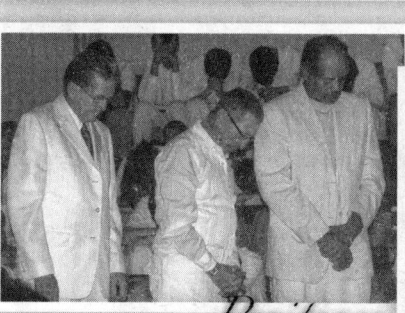

Penitence

Pure Worship

Strong Marriage

Celebrate God

You Can Do it

Pass it Down to the Next Generation

Prayer

Friendship

Blessings

Fellowship

Inexpressible Joy

BREAKTHROUGH

YOU HAVE MADE MANY BREAKTHROUGHS IN EIGHT WEEKS. NOW IS THE TIME TO KEEP GOING...

Weigh Down Ministries is the non-profit publishing house for and is sponsored by Remnant Fellowship Churches. It has been producing resources for over 30 years which have proven to help participants overcome overeating, alcoholism, gambling, drugs, sexual sins, materialism, and other strongholds, fully supporting all people seeking to glorify God and promote His Kingdom. If you need help or know someone who needs help, please refer to this list of resources.

Resources available at www.WeighDown.com

SEMINARS

The Treasure Series
NEXT, we suggest you take The Treasure Series, a 16-week seminar! An advanced study—based on nautical symbolism that helps the participant steer his ship in the right direction toward a deeper relationship with God. A deeper look into the world we live in, providing insight to what we truly treasure and adore.

Weigh Down Basics
This six-week beginning seminar teaches the foundational principles of Weigh Down.

Exodus Out of Egypt: The Change Series
This weight loss class goes beyond the basic foundational principles of Weigh Down Basics and The Last Exodus.

Exodus From Strongholds
12-week seminar. Break free from any stronghold in your life (overdrinking, nagging, anger, drugs, praise of man, shopping, control, smoking, etc.)—permanently.

The Last Exodus
Eight-week seminar for ages eight and up. Basic steps to help your children find a relationship with God.

History of the ONE TRUE GOD
A six-week in-depth study of the great love shown by God for all created beings and the appreciation due Him in return.

Weigh Down Advanced
   Ten-week seminar—discover the root of any remaining pull toward your strongholds and take your relationship with God to the next level. This opens your eyes to the big picture of how rebellion affects God and His Church.

Feeding Children Physically and Spiritually
   For children, parents, and parents-to-be—all will benefit from this information.

Zion Kids Series
   A collection of videos for elementary ages that will transform the whole household.

HEAR GWEN SHAMBLIN SPEAK LIVE

You Can Overcome TV Show
   Online weight loss TV show hosted by Gwen Shamblin every Wednesday at 6:20 p.m. Central Time. www.RemnantFellowship.TV.

Remnant Fellowship Services
   Visit a worship service at our founding location in Brentwood, Tennessee, or join us via webcast. Weekly worship services are held on Saturdays at 9:00 a.m. and Wednesdays at 6:00 p.m. Central Time. www.RemnantFellowship.org.

Weigh Down Radio
   Weigh Down Web Radio (WDWB)—Free 24/7 online encouragement. Join Gwen and others LIVE at 11:20 am Central—Monday, Tuesday and Thursday.

BOOKS, EBOOKS & AUDIO BOOKS

The Tablet
   Whether it is overeating, marriage problems or addictions, *The Tablet* offers step-by-step, clear, practical tips to putting God's principles into action, resulting in a completely victorious and transformed life. Also available in Ebook as a searchable, hyperlinked resource.

The Weigh Down Diet
   Original book by Gwen Shamblin, written in 1992. Practical advice to help you on the path from physical hunger to spiritual fulfillment.

BREAKTHROUGH Series

Rise Above
   A follow-up book to *The Tablet*... Look inward into your own heart and learn to transfer your devotion to the food over to a wholehearted devotion to God Almighty. Available in Ebook and Audio Book formats.

The Legend To The Treasure
   This book contains powerful spiritual lessons on how to lay down the last bit of self and praise of man, coupled with practical, true statistics of what life is like without God. Available in Ebook format.

History Of The One True God Volume I: The Origin Of Good And Evil
   Beautiful and clear account of Genesis Chapters One through Eight and how these events effect us to this very day. Available in Ebook and Audio Book formats.

WEBSITES & FREE RESOURCES

Truthstream
   A monthly online subscriber program where you have access to hundreds of life-changing audios and videos from Weigh Down.

WeighDown.com
   Visit our website for the most up-to-date information.

GwenShamblin.com
   More information on and pictures of the author, Gwen Shamblin.

RemnantFellowship.org
   More information on Remnant Fellowship Churches.

WeighDownatHome.com
   Free online weight loss materials to supplement your class.

WeighDownChronicles.com
   This free resource delivers encouraging devotionals to your email every weekday morning! It is a great way to start your day!

Facebook
   Join the Weigh Down Ministries Facebook Group—the 24/7 newsfeed is filled with testimonies, encouragement, and sharing.

Emails from Weigh Down
   Sign up today for Weigh Down's weekly encouragement emails at www.WeighDown.com.

Twitter
Follow "GwenShamblin," "WeighDown," "MichaelShamblin," and "ElizabethRFC" for tweets that will help you to stay focused.

YouTube
Watch inspiring videos on GwenShamblin, Remnant Fellowship Church, and MichaelShamblin YouTube Channels.

GwenShamblinBooks.com
Weekly excerpts from Gwen Shamblin's books sent via email.

MUSIC

For music that is guaranteed to turn your focus Heavenward, go to WeighDown.com or Michael Shamblin's YouTube channel or webpage, www.MichaelShamblin.com.

APPS FOR MOBILE DEVICES

Weigh Down App
Access with one click to Truthstream, Weigh Down Chronicles, TV Show, Remnant Fellowship webcasts, Weigh Down Radio, Weight Charts and more.

ADDITIONAL BREAKTHROUGH RESOURCES

Breakthrough Journal
This beautiful hardback spiral journal is perfect for taking notes during class.

Breakthrough Truth Cards
Receive 18 Truth cards with encouraging Scriptures and Truth that you can either keep on a key ring or in your purse.

Breakthrough Reinforcement Package
11 audio lessons, which are suggested as extra homework in this Breakthrough book. You will love the extra help and focus while you are in class.

Breakthrough: Talks that Move Your Heart
This audio package includes the most convicting audios, designed to move the most stubborn of hearts.

About the Author

Gwen Shamblin was born and raised in Memphis, Tennessee, with a strong faith and foundational values. She grew up with a medical background, making rounds with her belated father, Walter Henley, M.D., who was a General Surgeon. She received her undergraduate degree in Dietetics and Masters Degree in Nutrition with an emphasis in Biochemistry from the University of Tennessee in Knoxville. Gwen was an Instructor of Foods and Nutrition at the University of Memphis for five years, and she worked with the city's Health Department for an additional five years, helping specifically in the areas of overweight, obesity, pregnancy, and child health.

A very spiritual person with a strong faith in God, Gwen Shamblin felt led to found The Weigh Down Workshop in 1986 in order to teach these principles to those who were desperately seeking to lose weight permanently. Initially offered through audiotapes and small classes taught by Gwen in a retail setting, this teaching began yielding unprecedented results. Participants were not only losing their weight while eating regular foods, but they were using the same Bible-based principles to turn away from other strongholds such as smoking or alcohol abuse.

By 1992, the program was packaged for seminar use, churches began to sign up, and the media began to pay attention. The growth was explosive. By the late 1990s, Weigh Down was internationally known in most Protestant, Catholic, and Evangelical churches around the world. Gwen Shamblin and The Weigh Down Workshop were featured on such shows as *20/20*, *Larry King Live*, and *The View*, as well as in such magazines as *Good Housekeeping* and *Woman's Day*. In 1997, The Weigh Down Diet was published by Doubleday, Inc. The book quickly sold over one million copies as people discovered the secrets to losing weight quickly and permanently while finding a new relationship with God.

Feeling led to go even further in helping others to live fully for God, in 1999, Gwen Shamblin, along with other individuals who shared her passion for God, founded the Remnant Fellowship Church. Twice-weekly Church services are webcast live from the original Remnant Fellowship Church located outside Nashville, Tennessee.

Remnant Fellowship and Weigh Down Ministries have grown from the dream of helping people turn away from the love of food and toward a love of God. As a result of more than 30 years of counseling, Gwen has helped thousands of people break free from the pain of obesity, compulsive behaviors, and other dependencies. Gwen is continually producing new materials for both the Church and Weigh Down Ministries, yet she takes no salary for her efforts. Funds that are received through the sale of Weigh Down products and seminar fees or through donations to the Church are used to support each respectively in order to help hurting people of every nationality discover the love of God that can set them free.

Gabriele, Erin, Michael, Gates, and Garland Shamblin

Back row: Garland, Gweneth, Gabriele, Gracie, Charles Grantham. Front row: Gloria, Gates

Back row: Elizabeth, Gloria, and Brandon Hannah. Front row: Gweneth and Gracie Hannah.

Gwen has been married to David Shamblin for well over 30 years. They have two grown children who have children of their own. Their son, Michael, is married to Erin (Elle), and they have three daughters... Gabriele, Garland, and Gates. Gwen and David's daughter, Elizabeth, is married to Brandon Hannah, and they have four children... Gracie, Gweneth, Gloria, and Charles Grantham. The children and their spouses have always been supportive and work alongside her in the church and their contributions are invaluable.

211

BREAKTHROUGH

THE REMNANT FELLOWSHIP

The Remnant is not a new religion, but a continuation of what all the true Prophets of God have said from the beginning, as written in the Law and the Prophets, and made even more clear by Jesus Christ and the Apostles.

By 2000 AD, there was a clear deviation from the worship of God alone in churches across the land, and idolatry was rampant. A small group of devoted believers broke away from the established American Christianity at the turn of the century to re-establish the church based on the one fact that drove the message of all these Prophets: God is the sole Creator of the Universe and everything comes from Him and therefore He is the only one to be worshiped. God is Sovereign and reigns alone and has passed down His authority to His only Son, Jesus Christ. Jesus made it clear that He loved and bowed down to God alone, even through heavy testing in the desert. God has commanded that all should follow in Jesus' footsteps and adore and bow down to the Words that He spoke from the Father. God controls this world and all of our destinies. God is most merciful and loving, and it is His will that all would let Him lovingly rule. But the world is full of rebellion, yet all knees will eventually bow to God—whether voluntarily or on Judgment Day.

It is God's will that His church remains under His rule, so this small Remnant broke away to lay down rebellion and to start a church free from the false teachers (who falsely taught that we are helpless and sin will reign over our lives) and embrace the true teaching that we CAN break free from sin to worship and obey God alone! This message is powerful, and understanding this truth and accepting responsibility and personal accountability has changed our lives.

The Remnant does not teach blind faith. The people in the Remnant all changed from the established religious system to the Remnant for one reason: their entire lives (health, finances, and relationships) changed for the better because they found the truth about what God wanted for their lives. They had been living the lie about what God wanted, and once they found what He truly expected, they were blessed enormously for each change they made. This kind of blessing cannot be manufactured or faked, and it is not a form of theatrics. It is real. And we are offering the good news that will bless you so much and will be so obvious and ongoing that you will not be able to stop talking about it!

You can be a part of the Remnant no matter where you are or who you are! God has created technology and resources that allow us to connect all over the world. You will find Remnant members in countries all throughout the globe. God is growing His church. You can visit us anytime from wherever you are. Our Fellowship is strong and encouraging. We stay connected through webcasts, emails, phone calls, texts, and Facebook. God has made it easy to belong to this group regardless of your location!

It is time for a Change! The world is desperately seeking a Savior, and after generations of being misguided, misled, and abandoned, people are giving up. Give yourself and your family one more chance. Let Remnant Fellowship show you what a true, genuine, whole-hearted Christian life looks like—you will never be the same. If you are in our area, we would love to have you visit us in Brentwood, TN, or you can visit one of our many worldwide locations to join a webcast! (See contact information below.) We cannot wait to meet you. There is help and hope waiting for you!

How To Contact Us

Weigh Down Ministries
308 Seaboard Lane
Franklin, TN 37067
www.WeighDown.com
1-800-844-5208
info@weighdown.com

Remnant Fellowship
located at:
1230 Franklin Road
Brentwood, TN 37027

www.RemnantFellowship.org
www.RemnantFellowship.tv
www.YouTube.com—search Remnant Fellowship Church
www.RemnantFellowshipMinistries.com
RemnantNews.com
info@remnantfellowship.org